Traditions

Essays on the Japanese Martial Arts and Ways

Dave Lowry

TUTTLE Publishing

Tokyo | Rutland, Vermont | Singapore

The Tuttle Story: "Books to Span the East and West"

Most people are surprised to learn that the world's largest publisher of books on Asia had its beginnings in the tiny American state of Vermont. The company's founder, Charles E. Tuttle, belonged to a New England family steeped in publishing. And his first love was naturally books—especially old and rare editions.

Immediately after WW II, serving in Tokyo under General Douglas MacArthur, Tuttle was tasked with reviving the Japanese publishing industry, and founded the Charles E. Tuttle Publishing Company, which thrives today as one of the world's leading independent publishers.

Though a westerner, Charles was hugely instrumental in bringing a knowledge of Japan and Asia to a world hungry for information about the East. By the time of his death in 1993, Tuttle had published over 6,000 books on Asian culture, history and art—a legacy honored by the Japanese emperor with the "Order of the Sacred Treasure," the highest tribute Japan can bestow upon a non-Japanese.

With a backlist of over 1,500 titles, Tuttle Publishing is more active today as at any time in its past—inspired by Charles' core mission to publish fine books to span the East and West and provide a greater understanding of each.

Published by Tuttle Publishing,
an imprint of Periplus Editions (HK) Ltd.

www.tuttlepublishing.com

Copyright © 2002 Dave Lowry

Library of Congress Cataloging-in-Publication Data
Lowry, Dave.
      Traditions / Dave Lowry.
          p. cm.
      ISBN 0-8048-3432-6 (pbk.)
      1. Martial arts—Japan. I. Title.

      GV1100.77.L69 2002
      796.815—dc21
2002075921

ISBN 978-0-8048-3432-2

Design by Sheila Selden Design

Distributed by:

North America, Latin America & Europe
Tuttle Publishing
364 Innovation Drive
North Clarendon, VT 05759-9436 U.S.A.
tel: 1 (802) 773-8930, fax: 1 (802) 773-6993
info@tuttlepublishing.com
www.tuttlepublishing.com

Asia Pacific
Berkeley Books Pte Ltd
61 Tai Seng Avenue #02-12
Singapore 534167
tel: (65) 6280-1330, fax: (65) 6280-6290
inquiries@periplus.com.sg
www.periplus.com

Japan
Tuttle Publishing
Yaekari Building, 3F
5-4-12 Osaki, Shinagawa-ku
Tokyo 141-0032
tel: (81) 3 5437-0171, fax: (81) 3 5437-0755
sales@tuttle.co.jp
www.tuttle.co.jp

First edition
14 13 12 11   12 11 10 9 8
1111MP   Printed in Singapore

Traditions

Contents

An Introduction

In a corner of my home sits a baby's high chair that was already an antique when the first shots of the American Revolution were fired. (Yes, it *is* an odd way to begin writing about the Japanese martial arts and Ways. We will get to that presently; trust me.) When our child was a toddler he sat in the chair a few times, for special occasions. But this piece of furniture is a treasured possession for reasons far beyond its utility. It was made in New England, in the middle years of the 17th century. It is a singularly good example of the kind of simple, strong furniture the Puritans built during their first decades in this country, and though the chair is almost three centuries old, it is still sturdy and, to my way of thinking, quite beautiful.

I was fortunate to grow up in a home furnished and decorated with many reminders of early America like that baby chair. So in retrospect, it is natural, I suppose, I'd have an affinity to antiques. But more important than liking or enjoying them, my parents imbued me with a *respect* for old things. I learned to appreciate fine craftsmanship and quality of design because I was surrounded by it. I was taught that even though antiques were a functional part of our household, that I had a responsibility to take special care of them, to school myself in their attributes, and to be as certain as possible that they would be correctly preserved for future generations.

While I was still young, I was equally fortunate to become exposed to the *budo*, the martial arts and Ways of Japan. These arts set the guideposts for a path that I have been following for over one quarter of a century now, a path that continues to be rewarding and profound to me. I cannot claim that the various sensei and seniors under whom I learned were the most skilled exponents in the budo. Nor even especially well-known. But they were outstanding teachers and mentors and I am still learning from some of them. The training and teaching they offered were as enjoyable as anything I have ever done. It continues to be so today. It was also strict at times, and tedious, and for the most part, it was conducted along lines that were traditional and not much affected by current trends and ideas. I learned the lessons of the budo the same way my teachers had learned them; the same way their teachers learned before them.

Just as are most people drawn to these arts, particularly young people, my original intentions were to learn the budo in the hope of becoming adept at protecting myself from the dangers, real and imagined (and a teenage boy had at that time just as he does now, a quantity of both), that life holds. Over time, I began to discover that "self-defense" is almost an incidental by-product of these arts. It was impressed upon me that their ultimate goals were to be found instead, in different realms, in arenas that were by no means obvious at first glance, or even observable at all from the perspective of the outsider. I discovered, in short, what all serious practitioners find eventually, that the goals of the budo lie in the refinement of the body and the spirit.

Yet, possibly because of my childhood among antiques, and probably because of the encouragement of my sensei, I came to see something else in my budo training. The martial arts and Ways of Japan, I have come to think, are an intimate and powerful connection with the past. Within their techniques and methods and rituals are the essence of the well-lived life as their practitioners of old saw it, and as such they can be considered artifacts every bit as valuable as the antiques in any museum. In his etiquette, his traditions, and philosophies, we can know what was important to the martial artist of the feudal era. Combining the lessons of the physical training in the budo he has left us, along with a perspective on his intellectual and spiritual outlook then, affords today's exponent a link with another age that is significant, remarkably so.

Sixteen years ago, when I was preparing for a trip to Japan to further my study of the budo and of Japanese culture, I got a call from the editor of *Black Belt Magazine*. Would I be interested in writing a monthly column on the traditional aspects of karate and the budo in general? I was surprised at the offer. At that time, the "martial arts" in the United States were dominated by violent films and by gaudy public exhibitions and contests. A number of innovators were creating new forms of self-defense and personal combat that had been freed from the "classical mess" of the past. The martial disciplines were becoming "Westernized," which was allegedly an improvement for them and which was going to make them more meaningful or at least more palatable to the non-Japanese enthusiast. Concepts like budo philosophy or traditional training methods were either being ignored or dismissed as archaic or categorized as that most egregious of failings in this end of the present century: irrelevant. I could not imagine much of a readership for such a column. But I took the offer anyway. And as it has been more than once in my writing career, my editor was correct. I began to hear from readers in response to my columns.

I learned, in writing about the traditions of the budo on a regular basis, that there was a wide readership of intrigued individuals who were taking a deeper look at the budo, understanding that there may be something of value in these Ways, not immediately evident. Not incidentally, the same has come to be true on the antiques scene. Newly involved collectors are discovering that what they previously regarded as old trash, may be a connecting element to earlier times and the ownership of these objects can bring satisfaction and even a certain stability to daily life.

The sincere martial artist shares at least one other similarity with the antiques enthusiast. Both must traipse through a lot of junk and a lot of imitations before they find the real thing. Age alone does not elevate a thing to the status of antique, nor does its immediate appearance guarantee quality. Likewise, there are plenty of martial arts (and what have been ambitiously or fraudulently labeled as martial arts) that have been practiced for years, despite the fact that they're largely nonsense. There are many imitations that can look most convincing, even if they are not authentic.

It is discouraging. But those who have a real interest in the budo as they were originally practiced have a responsibility to understand them as well, so that these wonderful Ways may be accurately preserved, like my Puritan chair, for future generations. That has been the audience for my writing over the past ten years. I hear from them frequently, when I have made a mistake or when they disagree with something I have written. I am happy to say, however, that far more often, readers write to tell me they have enjoyed the columns and have learned from them.

"I always knew there was a lot more to the martial arts than what I was learning," one reader told me, "and your column has encouraged me to investigate." These sentiments, expressed in one way or another over the years, have left me with the feeling experienced by the antique collector who, through his own enthusiasm, inspires others to begin appreciating the things of the past. That is what my writing in these columns has been about, in a real sense. Poking about in the attic of the budo, bringing down the interesting and intriguing odds and ends to be found there, to show them to others who share my preoccupations. I have been encouraged by readers to collect some of these columns and to publish them in the more manageable and presentable form of a book. I have, and that is what you are reading now.

Some of these essays deal in broad terms with the traditions of the budo; others are concerned specifically with the Way of karate. I hope that those martial artists whose Way is not that of karate and who instead practice aikido, kendo, judo, or some other budo, will read these anyway for two reasons. One, I believe that karate, more so than the other budo, has suffered badly at the hands of Hollywood and others intent upon presenting it as a brutal form of violence, a machismo-flavored soupcon of egotism and boorishness. Karate is much, much more than most Westerners (and regrettably I include most Western karateka in that group) understand it to be. It is partially my intention here to present some of its philosophy and ethos.

Secondly, I think it is important for martial artists to realize that all the budo are, at their core, alike. They are, to think of it in a different way, various climbing routes up the same mountain. Several excellent (and some perfectly lousy) books have been written detailing the climbing routes of aikido or the Way of the sword or some of the other Japanese budo. But the Western reader interested in karate's particular path to the summit has had little to go on. Perhaps these essays will provide some insights for him and for other martial artists. In any case, it is my intention that this modest collection will reveal at least a few glimpses of the traditions that make up all of the Japanese budo.

They are unique, the budo, modern forms of self-discipline and aesthetic sensibility and moral reckoning with deep and powerful roots in an ancient age. They offer a lifetime of study and effort and contemplation. Neither my writing, nor any other, is going to build a foundation for you that will allow you to benefit from these Ways. That is a process that can only be accomplished through your own severe and dedicated efforts in concert with the guidance of a competent teacher or guide. Instead of a foundation, I present here for you a little corner of the attic, one filled with antiquities and curiosities. I offer this little space under the eaves for you to explore, in the sincere wish that you will find something of interest and worth. Something like the baby chair of the Puritan Age that I have, some things which are worth taking down and studying and appreciating and making into a part of your daily life.

The Spears of Hozoin

"Any instant is the same as thousands of infinite eons.
And thousands of infinite eons are the same as a single instant."
—*Kegon-kyo* ("The Sutra of Flowered Splendor")

From its outward appearances, this temple-monastery was little different from others of the Buddhist faith throughout 17th-century Japan. It contained a main *dojo*, or votive room, with a great wooden effigy of the Buddhist patriarch Tojun in the center of its altar. There were spacious abbot's quarters, and other buildings for the monks, retired abbots, and those who frequented such temples in their travels. Spaced throughout the grounds were the customary gardens, their perfectly placed stones and cultivated trees intermingled with more prosaic varieties of growing things useful to a monastery of hungry holy men: *daikon* radishes, scallions, beans, and other vegetables.

There were some characteristics distinguishing this temple. It was one dedicated to the Kegon sect of Buddhism, which accounted for the statue of Tojun, known in China as To-shun, one of the religion's primogenitors. It was favorably located on the crest of steep Abura Hill, in the shady middle of a grove of evergreen cryptomeria that funneled the coolest breezes of summer over its walls and sheltered the temple too, from the harshest gusts of winter. Looking out in one direction from the temple walls, one could spy the tiled roof of a public bathhouse in the forest below, one that had been commissioned in the 14th century by the Empress Komyo. From another vantage point, the towering outline of Mt. Kasuga loomed. Then too, this particular temple had a certain "air" about it. The sharp scent of pepper to be exact. The temple was famous for the spicy pickled vegetables its monks fermented in wooden vats in their kitchen. Yet what really set this temple apart from others was the long bladed poles that were stored under the eaves of the monk's quarters, their oaken shafts polished with use, their steel edges kept razored with care. For this temple was the Hozoin, and its monks were the feared and respected spearmen of the Hozoin ryu, one of ancient Japan's most feared schools of spearmanship.

The Hozoin was consecrated to the Kegon sect of Buddhism. Kegon, known as Hua-yen in Chinese, was formalized in China very early in the T'ang Dynasty (618–907 A.D.). Kegon sprouted at almost exactly the same time another school of Chinese Buddhism came into prominence, the Chan or Zen sect, and in many ways, Kegon was an intellectual approach to Buddhism, complementing the more spontaneous methods of Zen. Kegon drew its inspiration from the *Avatamsaka* sutra, a sacred text that based enlightenment upon adherence to the principles of the Ten Mysterious Gates. In simplified form, the doctrines of Kegon maintain that all existence is dependent upon a vast, interlocking network of karma, or personal actions. In Kegon thought, the universe is like an enormous machine, one with millions upon millions of cogs, each of them turning in relation to all the others. Enlightenment comes to the Kegon practitioner when he realizes independence is illusory and that existence is an ultimate interdependence upon others, past and present. And so, the follower of Kegon Buddhism seeks to integrate himself into the world, understanding the greater scheme of things by understanding his own little cog.

Exactly when Kegon Buddhism was imported to Japan is a mystery. But by the 16th century, there were several temples there dedicated to it. One of these was in Nara, named the Hozo, after the Japanese pronunciation of Fa-tsang, the Chinese priest who formalized Kegon teachings. For many years, the Hozoin monks lived in simple solitude, making their renowned pickles and contemplating the scriptures of Kegon thought. It wasn't until about 1620, with the appointment of Kakuzenbo Innei as chief abbot, that things began to change.

Innei had been, like many other clergymen in feudal Japan, the younger son of a large family. Denied by custom any of his family's estate and faced with a life of poverty, he entered the priesthood while still virtually a child. He applied himself to a study of the canons of Kegon faith, the Sanskrit *Gandavyuha* sutra and the Chinese *Chin-shi-tsu-chang*, and was rewarded, while still quite young, with an advancement to the post of abbot. The position meant many new duties, but it also allowed him an opportunity to pursue a lifelong dream, a strange one for a priest. Kakuzenbo Innei immersed himself in the deadly art of swordsmanship. With his temple's political connections, he was able to become the friend and student of Kitabatake Tomonori, the governor of Ise Province and a master fencer of the

Kashima Shinto ryu. Later, he undertook a study of the Katori Shinto ryu, under the teaching of Onishiki Shunken.

As his years of training piled up, however, Innei became more and more interested in a corollary art of both ryu, the methods of the spear, called *sojutsu*. The young priest concentrated his energies on the spear, polishing his skill and gradually incorporating his own ideas into his practice. On afternoons after the day's devotional liturgy were finished, the air of the temple courtyard hummed as Innei's spear cut through it in sojutsu's precise thrusts and sweeps. It wasn't long before many of the monks watching Innei begged their abbot to teach, and thus was born the Hozoin ryu.

By the mid-1500s, the Hozoin had become a pilgrimage site, not just for members of the Kegon sect, but for wandering martial artists as well, who wished to test their abilities. According to legend, a young, aspiring swordsman named Miyamoto Musashi paid a visit to the temple. In reality, through the gates of the Hozoin passed many of that age's greatest martial arts masters. Yagyu Muneyoshi and his son, Yagyu Munenori, founders of the Yagyu Shinkage school of fencing, were acquaintances of the master Innei. Okuyama Kimishige, headmaster of the Okuyama ryu, visited, as did Ono Jiroemon Tadaaki, second headmaster of the Itto ryu, and Toda Shigemasa, of the Toda style of swordsmanship. For so small a temple as the Hozo to have been the center of so much exalted attention, not to mention the hordes of lesser known warriors who journeyed there for a match or lesson, the methods of the ryu must have been truly impressive. Unfortunately, we know comparatively little of the Hozoin spear techniques. There is a Hozoin ryu still in existence, but its movements have been changed considerably. About twenty kata with the spear used in the manner of the Hozoin ryu are still extant, most of them featuring the school's most distinctive technique. This involves thrusting the blade and tip of the spear toward the joints of an opponent's body, at the knee, for example, or under the arm, and then twisting the weapon forcefully in a circular motion that bends the joint, throwing the opponent as neatly as any judo throw.

This unusual method of sojutsu was possible for the spearman of the ryu because he used a particular weapon sometimes referred to as a Hozoin *yari* (spear). The Hozoin yari had a crescent-shaped hook fixed at right angles to the shaft a couple of feet down from the point. The wide crescent helped to entangle an attacker and kept him from moving any closer to the spearman.

Historians generally agree that the Hozoin yari was an adaptation of spears used by aboriginal Ainu bear hunters in the far northern province of Hokkaido. The Ainu would attach a crossbar to their weapons so a bear, already impaled on the point, couldn't force itself down the shaft in its dying anguish, killing the hunter. But a popular tale gives a different rendering to the Hozoin spear's creation.

The story has it that a young man from a nearby village came to the Hozoin seeking admittance to become a monk. His family was impoverished, but he was healthy and exceptionally strong, and although he had a reputation as being rather strong willed as well, the monks took pity on him. They accepted him as a servant, often the position taken by aspirants to the priesthood. Most of these novices accepted their temporary lot. They performed the various menial tasks they were assigned, looking forward to the day when they might join the ranks of the other monks. Young Matsu, however, was not content with waiting. He worked at a demon's pace, finishing an entire day's jobs in a couple of hours. He was up before the most faithful and was still hard at it when the last candle was extinguished at night. Even so, after two weeks of such frantic activity, his efforts had not earned him so much as an encouraging smile from his seniors.

Angry at what he perceived as a snub, Matsu changed his tactics in a bold way. While his family was poor, they were among the ranks of the *jizamurai,* farmers who, in times of need, had served their lords as warriors. When he was little more than a toddler, Matsu's father had taught him to hold and thrust a spear. It didn't occur to him that the spear his father had shown him how to use was nothing but a broken rake handle. Matsu had practiced the basic moves of spearmanship for most of his life. He was not intimidated by the reputation of the fighting Hozoin monks. Brazenly, he approached a senior who was supervising training one morning, and made his challenge. The monk, thinking to pound some sense into the boy, gave him a practice spear and took a stance against him. Incredibly, Matsu screamed and charged, smashing a wicked blow against the forehead of the monk, who did not regain consciousness for an hour, by which time the entire temple buzzed with accounts of the incident.

Some of the monks thought Matsu might be a child prodigy. They had their best spearmen face him. These were expert warriors, accustomed to all the maneuvers and stances of the various schools of the martial arts. But they were taken completely off-guard by the unorthodox yet devastating way Matsu leaped at them, brushing their weapons aside and raining blows down clumsily and painfully upon them. Innei himself witnessed the final two of these "duels." He addressed the losers firmly.

"You have been too easy on the boy," he said. "He defeated you because you were so concerned with not hurting him. Tomorrow," he said, "I will see to putting an end to his arrogance."

Innei suspected his students weren't really so poor they could be defeated by a servant. Wanting to punish Matsu for his insolence, they nevertheless had no desire to endanger his life. Indeed, Innei realized he'd put himself in the same predicament. The only way he could show Matsu the error of his ways was to risk killing him, hardly a worthy act for a Buddhist abbot. In a quandary, Innei spent the evening in his garden, moving about with the spear. He continued his exercise, even when clouds billowed up in the nighttime sky, crackling with the energy of a coming storm. Lost in thought, Innei stood on the bank of a small pond, watching the reflection of his spear as he swung it over the dark water. That is when inspiration appeared, the story goes, quite literally in a flash of illumination. A finger of lightning streaked across the sky, reflecting off the surface of the pond, and appearing to cross the shaft of Innei's spear.

The next morning, in one of the Hozoin's gardens, Innei and Matsu squared off with practice spears. But instead of a straight polearm, Innei's yari had a curved crossbar of wood fixed tightly to the shaft with cord. A more experienced martial artist would have paused to consider this modification. Changing even a few inches of the length of a weapon could mean a drastic difference in the way it was used. Matsu ignored the results of Innei's inspiration, though. He rushed at the abbot, his spear clutched in his hand. His face was ablaze with determination to prove himself worthy of the priesthood, or at least to gain some attention. In response, Innei pushed his spear up, catching Matsu at the knees with the crosspiece. Then, with a twist, the abbot flung him into the air. Matsu crashed at the feet of the monks assembled to watch the match. Innei slowly walked over to the fallen boy and stood over him to check for any damage. "You must learn to be patient," he said. "Rushing into the priesthood will work no better than rushing in against a warrior."

If we are to believe the story, Matsu took the counsel seriously. So much so that he went on to become the second headmaster of the ryu, achieving almost as much fame in his time as Innei had received in his.

Is the tale of the Hozoin spear's inspiration in the reflection of lightning in a pond true? Or just a legend? It is impossible to tell. But there is no doubt at all that the most renowned school of the spear in old Japan was not founded by great samurai or noble warriors. Its creation is owed to the monks of an otherwise insignificant temple on the southeastern edge of Nara. So lasting was their reputation, in fact, that even today priests of all Buddhist sects all over Japan are sometimes referred to by the title of *Osho*. It is a title that has nothing to do with their religious calling. Instead, it means, "Honorable Teacher of the Spear."

Ryomi (Reflection)

"In following the ways of the warrior, see that you yourself are right. Then you may think of defeating others."

—*Innei Kakuzenbo*

Kofujita Kangejuzaemon Toshinao was a master swordsman of the feudal age in Japan, one whose entire life was dedicated to his craft. His apprenticeship in fencing began under a teacher of the Chujo ryu. While still a boy, though, Kofujita was accepted into the dojo of Itto Ittosai Kagehisa, the founder of the Itto or "One Sword" style of martial strategy.

The tactics of the Itto ryu called for a daring sense of timing and an absolute confidence in an ability to make a single, expertly executed technique at precisely the right moment. It was an approach to swordsmanship that Kofujita took to with enthusiasm. When his master Ittosai was off on one of his many journeys in search of worthwhile opponents (or dallying with a variety of the mistresses he kept, in search of something perhaps even more worthwhile), Kofujita practiced under the school's seniormost student, Ono Tadaaki. It was Ono who fired the young Kofujita with a feeling of purpose and duty. Kofujita took seriously Ono's lectures about filial loyalty and duty. When a local noble cheated Kofujita's aged father in a business matter, Kofujita, barely in his teens, took up the cause. He confronted eight of the nobleman's samurai along the street one afternoon. According to legends handed down within the ryu, he killed two of them and wounded three others before the rest hastily retreated.

As he matured, Kofujita became a bit calmer and more circumspect. Yet he never lost his enthusiasm for swordsmanship and for perfecting his technique in the art. He worked tirelessly for years on the basics of the Itto style of fencing. He taught many students of his own and in time came to be recognized as an authority on swordsmanship and as a *shihan*, literally, a "model for all others." Not long before Kofujita's master, Ittosai, retired from teaching, he gave Kofujita permission to open his own school. Ittosai seemed to realize that Kofujita was enough a master in his own right that his contributions allowed him to found an offshoot of the Itto style, which Kofujita christened the Yuishin Itto ryu.

One day Kofujita was out practicing in his garden when a visitor stopped by to see him, an old friend who'd grown up with him and had trained at the Itto dojo. A servant led the friend into the garden where Kofujita was standing alone, barely moving, just lifting the sword in his hands up a few inches and letting it drop, twisting his hips slightly. The friend saw that Kofujita was practicing at using his hips to precede the action of striking. It was the very first lesson an Itto ryu swordsman learned upon entering training. He wondered why a brilliant master like Kofujita was so intently working at this simple exercise. As he drew closer, however, he saw that the master was furiously at it, his whole being centered on the motion. When Kofujita looked up at his old friend, there were tears in his eyes.

"The first technique our master Ittosai taught us," he said, his voice choked with emotion. "I don't think it is quite good enough yet, do you?"

Kofujita's introspection, his incessant willingness to critically observe his progress, reflect upon it, and strive for improvement no matter how long he'd practiced or how perfect his technique is a characteristic of the master budoka. This attitude is called *ryomi* in Japanese. Ryomi is an intense, ongoing process of self-evaluation for the martial artist or anyone else who hopes to make something worthwhile of his life.

Within the modern budo, "traditionalist" is a label affixed to those who adhere to the ways of the past. You will not find them wearing glitzy training clothes, or indulging their egos at tournaments. They follow the path of the budo because they see it as a journey of self-discovery, one that will only be frustrated by indulging in fads. They believe they are correct in their attitudes, and so they are an obstinate bunch, the sort of people whom the British would refer to admiringly as "hard ones." I respect these individuals very much, and it is flattering to note that by the correspondence I receive, that some readers even think of me as a traditionalist. It occurs that some might have the impression that traditionalists regard themselves as faultless paragons, noble paladins of the Ways of the warrior. This is an impression rarely challenged by the traditionalist himself who, if he engages in any form of self-criticism at all, invariably does it in secrecy, among his own kind.

The kind of martial artist we refer to as a traditionalist can be forgiven for this deficiency in his character. It is not easy, after all, for traditionalists to analyze their own faults, for a couple of reasons. The most obvious one is that the complexities and depths of the budo forms they follow far exceed the "eclectic" fighting arts that have been created recently. It is tempting to become complacent. Budoka learning under the tutelage of experts can see firsthand the immense power and skill possessed by their teachers. Frankly, many of them simply cannot imagine that anything could possibly be bad about a system that turns out such masters. A second reason why many traditionalists don't spend much time in the contemplative process of ryomi is that the criticism of their arts is by and large, inutterably ignorant. "What's all that kata stuff got to do with real fighting?" ponders some self-appointed critic, who might just as well ask an auto mechanic what value a drive shaft plays in making a car go. Under such less than inspired criticism and with no real competition in the physical sense, it's understandable that the traditionalist might get the idea that he's a purist, the consummate example, faultless.

He is not. And if a master like Kofujita Toshinao could submit himself to the self-criticism of ryomi, then today's budoka could survive and maybe even benefit from a little of the same.

The overall problem faced by the traditionalist is that while his world is filled with excellence, it is far too small. Often its dimensions extend only to the walls of his dojo. There his exposure is limited to others who train in his particular art, taught by only a few select teachers. This makes for a highly accomplished karateka or judoka or whatever. But it can also foster an individual of rather narrow views. The karate student needn't try to widen his world by collecting the sprains and bruises of kendo; the judoka doesn't have to accustom himself to the different sort of throws encountered in aikido. But there is nothing inherently sinful in karateka, judoka, kendoka, and aikidoka spending time at one another's dojo, observing the training, asking questions, and getting to know traditionalists of the other arts. If they do, they will not be breaking tradition. They will be following an old and valuable custom in the budo.

None of the Japanese budo developed in a vacuum. Judo's founder, Jigoro Kano, sent some of his best students to the dojo of karate master Gichin Funakoshi so they could learn his newly imported karate. Kano later introduced some of karate's striking techniques into the kata of judo. The legendary Okinawan karate expert Yabu Kentsu studied judo continuously during his years of service in the Japanese army, and when he returned to Okinawa he often amazed his students with his ability to incorporate throws during training in the karate dojo.

Today this kind of interchange is sadly lacking. When I visit a typical budo dojo, I am often reminded of the spirit of provincialism that now seems to dominate the thinking in these Ways. Now, no one expects an aikidoka to be able to punch like a skilled karate exponent. Even so, I have seen aikido students who couldn't even make a proper fist. Likewise, it's common to see karateka go down against a footsweep, yet how often can they control and protect themselves with proper *ukemi* (falling methods)? If the karateka can show an aikidoka the correct way to make a fist, if the judoka is willing to teach the karateman to fall without injury, everyone benefits. In the course of such exchanges, a great deal of understanding about one's own Way can be gained.

In the traditionalist's small world, his sensei achieves a status difficult for the outsider to comprehend. In daily training the traditional budoka is pressed to do things that go against his every instinct: standing compliantly while an opponent practices control by blasting punches just brushing his nose, allowing himself to be thrown flying, continuing on long after his body has told him to stop. These are accomplished only by trusting his sensei implicitly. In return, the student is molded into a budoka, given a life beyond the neuroses and psychological limitations that hobble much of the rest of the modern world.

The serious budoka never for a second forgets the debt he owes for this. He treats his teacher with endless respect, loves him, and considers his advice priceless and undebatable. This is exactly how it has always been and how it should be. If one of my own sensei told me that I could only improve my technique by practicing underwater, you can believe I'd start looking for a sale on aqualungs. But if my sensei told me to invest all my savings in the nuclear-powered lawn mower industry, you can also rest assured that I would consult with stockbrokers and other financial analysts before I sunk my money into such a venture. Unfortunately, too many traditionalists fail to make this distinction. They prefer to perceive their teacher as a father figure, infallible in every situation and with absolute answers to everything from how to dress to whom one should marry.

The sensei, most of them Japanese, cannot be blamed for this. From the moment they landed here to introduce the martial arts to the West, they have been treated like royalty. They were never questioned when appointing themselves head of each major budo organization, and since their students showed little inclination to do things on their own, the Japanese masters were quick to establish themselves as administrators, governing every facet of these organizations. One Caucasian karateman recalls how the national meetings of a prominent karate group were held back in the sixties. "We'd have an open table discussion with a lot of good, contrasting ideas presented by knowledgeable members, and we'd vote. It was all very democratic. Sensei would listen to it all, then he'd tell us what was going to be done."

By analogy, imagine what would happen if a prima donna ballet dancer were to appear at a meeting of the board of directors of a dance company, telling them how the company's funds were to be allocated, how they should conduct business, and so on. The prima donna might be a peerless dancer. Her performing and instructing are wonderful assets for the dance company. Yet no one assumes that she is automatically also a brilliant administrator. The same holds true for the martial arts masters. They are unbelievably, awesomely skilled; in terms of the budo they are a priceless source of information. We here in the West are most fortunate to have them teaching us. But to have them running national budo organizations where thousands of members and millions of dollars are involved, especially when some of those members are experts in financial and business management and have their skills go unused, is a waste. It allows for decisions to be made on the basis of old college rivalries back in Japan, on philosophical evaluations that do not enter into business interests, and on a whole system of management that's more like that of a feudal ryu than a modern organization supposedly bent on improving and spreading a budo. Western martial artists should strive always to show respect for their sensei. They should see to it that the sensei is paid well, in accordance with his high position and profession. And they should have no qualms whatsoever about assuming control of their organizations in an equally professional way. In addition to being a big step in the maturation of the senior American budoka, this is quite probably the only course by which the martial Ways can survive and grow on a widespread basis in the West.

Traditionalists do not need me to point out these specific problems, nor should they be upset at having them made public. Because they have been taught so well, they can seek out their own weaknesses. Since their art is strong, they need not fear having their shortcomings brought out for others to see. In fact, they should welcome the opportunity to reflect in the honored traditions of ryomi, just as masters like Kofujita Kangejuzaemon of the Yuishin Itto ryu did. Ryomi is a process as grueling as any physical training, and one just as important in the education of the traditional budoka.

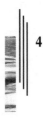

A Puppy Dog's Bark

The date: around 1630 probably. The place: a little *nomiya*, a rustic shack of a restaurant that served travelers in that rural corner of central Japan. The afternoon's business: slow. Heat oozed in from off the dusty highway outside. The greasy *noren* (a split length of cloth serving as an informal doorway) was unruffled by even the faintest breeze. Inside, except for the flies droning, the only customers were a pair of itinerant barbers and a swordsman. The latter sat near the window, watching the empty highway with a sleepy sort of disinterest and sucking noisy mouthfuls of cold noodles from a cheap bowl. Because he smelled and looked more than a little in need of a bath and scratched most distastefully with the blunt ends of his chopsticks at the scruffy patch of eczema on his forehead, the barbers did their best to ignore him.

Presently, the noren parted. Three young *ronin* ambled in, dusty and blinking in the darkness of the nomiya, their eyes still accustomed to the bright sun outside. They gave their orders in curt, tired voices to the proprietor who in turn snapped irritably at his assistant. Only after they had slumped wearily onto the floor matting and been served tea did they notice the swordsman by the window. Perhaps it was because they were shamed by the quality of the swords they carried. Ronin were men of samurai rank who, for one reason or another, were not in the service of a lord. They tended to be an uncouth lot. Looking at the fine weapon of the other diner, perhaps they felt a need to display their toughness. Probably, however, the young ronin were just hot and tired and ill-tempered, and the odd-looking swordsman was an easy target for their teasing.

One of the ronin began slurping his tea loudly, mocking the swordsman, who continued to slurp his noodles. The others laughed, and another of them grabbed at the hair above his own forehead and mussed it wildly, mocking the swordsman's unsightly skin condition, while the third rolled his eyes.

"Whew," he growled, "that one smells like a wild pig."

Neither of the two barbers who were also eating in the nomiya had ever so much as held a sword. But with all the caution of master warriors they watched the swordsman. No one of his rank, they knew, would allow these kinds of insults to pass unheeded. Though they remained quiet, eating with mechanical slowness, they were ready to leap for the doorway at the first sign of a fight lest they become caught in the melee sure to ensue.

By now each of the three ronin had casually touched the swords beside them, with the pretense of adjusting their position slightly. Actually, each had pushed the collar of his sword free from the scabbard by an inch or two, freeing the blades for the fastest use possible. Ready now, they waited.

The flies buzzed in lazy loops, scouting the noodles below.

"Hey, ugly," barked one of the ronin. "Wouldn't you be better off out in back with the other—" his jest was cut off by the movement of the swordsman, who looked up from his bowl for the first time. His head swiveled. His eyes followed the droning flies. Then, like some kind of mantis, he struck.

"Click . . . Click, click." Between the pincers of his chopsticks three flies were crushed with a speed that did not seem real.

A long stillness filled the air of the nomiya. Finally, there were three more clicks. It was the sound of the ronin carefully snapping their swords back into their scabbards. They finished their own meals with the politest of silences. The swordsman, the son of a Harima Province constable and known as Miyamoto Musashi, continued to slurp his cold noodles.

The famous story of Musashi and the three ronin is, disappointingly, more a legend than anything like a documented event. Like many of the other stories of his life, it may not ever have happened. But if it did, it is a good example of what martial artists have always respected as one of the aims of the budo. What Musashi understood in the threat of the ronin at the nomiya was the distinction between two kinds of attacks that martial artists (as well as the rest of the population, for that matter) should always be aware of. This distinction might be more aptly demonstrated in a contemporary setting.

A young Japanese karate exponent and his wife were visiting New York City a few years ago. They'd met some friends at a Manhattan restaurant for dinner and after eating they left the restaurant in search of a taxi to take them back to their hotel. Standing on a street corner in many parts of Manhattan can be an unnerving experience at any time, of course. But when it is nearly midnight and your hometown is on the other side of the earth, it can be particularly trying.

The couple had nearly reached the conclusion that every taxi driver in that part of the city was extracting revenge for Japan's sin of having produced a fuel efficient car. At least half a dozen of them breezed past without so much as a glance in their direction. Abruptly, the couple's problem was compounded.

"Hey, China Doll! You lookin' *nice*." An admirer sauntered up to lean against a street lamp. He mouthed remarks insulting to the man and insinuating to his wife, both of whom pretended not to understand. The wife moved so that her husband was between herself and the stranger. The situation grew more tense. The jerk stepped away from the light post. "Come on, pretty lady. I'll show you a real good time." He reached his arm out in front of the husband. "This Jap ain't gonna be no fun," he said.

The jerk didn't know it, but the "Jap" in question had achieved something of a reputation back in Japan for snapping off the *makiwara* punching posts in his dojo when he struck them. If he'd hit the troublesome jerk, there was a real possibility he'd have inflicted terrible, perhaps fatal damage. Instead, he laughed. Uproariously. He gave the man a playful shove, the kind a friend might give another, rocking the jerk back on his heels.

"You wouldn't want to spend any time with her," he said, still laughing and, with his arm around his wife, turning to walk toward a taxi he saw down the block. "She's a Jap, too!"

It is unlikely that Musashi or the karateka in Manhattan would have had much trouble if they'd chosen to reply to their aggravators in a physical way. Both were experts in lethal techniques of fighting. Yet both of them solved potentially explosive situations by resorting to stratagems that hurt no one. Many of us would have been driven to react to these kinds of threats. We would have been tempted to respond aggressively in either case, particularly if we were reasonably certain of winning. Why then, did those two not?

Musashi and the karateka both avoided a violent altercation because in both instances, each realized the attacks directed at them were attacks against their ego, their self-image, rather than against themselves or those around them. The mocking taunts of the ronin may have embarrassed Musashi (though he was ragged and dirty much of his life, his self-portrait is one of a man dressed in fine clothes, evidence of Musashi's pride). They were far from being a threat to his safety. The karateka certainly could not have enjoyed the lewd remarks made to his wife. But by his response he not only showed the crude stranger how idiotic his advances were, he also demonstrated his mastery of the budo by settling a potential conflict without resorting to violence.

Had the two martial artists pursued the course many would have taken, consider the results. The three ronin—as well as the bystanders possibly—would have been killed or injured. In the karateka's situation, he might have been able to control his blows. Still, suppose, as happened in an altercation in St. Louis recently, the offending man had fallen when the karateka hit him, had struck his head against the curb, and died as a result. Lives would have been taken or irretrievably lessened, and all because of some name-calling.

It would be a mistake to assume that Musashi and the karateka, because they avoided violence in these instances, would not ever have resorted to fighting. If the streetcorner punk had grabbed the karateka's wife or physically assaulted him, the results would have been immediate and, for the assailant, unforgettable. Musashi killed dozens of opponents on the battlefield or in duels. Yet because of their training, both men responded in a way that left no one injured or killed since they saw that neither situation warranted it.

Distinguishing between an attack on our egos and an actual physical assault is easy to determine in retrospect. When confronted with the actual circumstances, the difference can be blurred by anger or fear. When my driving elicits an obscene gesture from someone in another car, my immediate impulse is to become equally angry and to return the gesture or shout. But if I think for only a moment, I realize my anger is probably due to the fact that I *am* a lousy driver (to which anyone who's ever ridden with me will attest). The other motorist, by bringing it so rudely to my attention, is taking a poke at my ego that is difficult to ignore. While an average sized person standing in a line might think nothing of a jostle from behind, the skinny fellow beside him might well be quick to return the shove back out of the fear that, because of his diminutive size and equally frail ego, he is being threatened.

No one likes being teased or ridiculed. When we consider that the common response, to reply with equal or greater vigor, is what causes wars between nations, we realize that we need to consider other solutions. For the budoka, at least one of those solutions is found in the dojo. He finds one answer in the kind of constant, intensive training that allows him to defend himself physically should that be necessary. But he finds another solution, one which more practically strips away false pretensions and fears and fragile or bloated egos and instead leaves him with a feeling of quiet pride and self-worth that is invulnerable. The man or woman who has persevered daily, monthly, yearly through the demands placed upon them by budo training knows that they have endured unique experiences, passed tests of spirit and soul and body. With these experiences comes a knowledge that permits them to smile and to shrug off assaults on their ego as easily as Musashi killed the flies.

The ability to perceive the difference between a shot at our self-image and a dangerous attack on our self, our family, or our society and to respond accordingly is an unmistakable sign of budo mastery. As one of my sensei once so eloquently put it, "You cannot concern yourself about every little puppy dog that barks at you. Worry yourself only with those that mean to bite."

5

The First Attack Position and Other Lessons from the Paperback Ryu

It is the novel's climactic fight scene, finally. After more than 300 pages or so, filled with all kinds of intrigue in foreign and domestic places, well-placed descriptions of graphic and presumably exotic romantic encounters, and lots of clinically detailed violence, we have reached the moment where the good guy meets the bad. Larynxes have been lacerated; sternums shattered, and there is swordplay, with lots of *katana* that glitter and flicker and sparkle in the adjective-rich lexicon of the author. Page after page, bodies are dismembered, hacked, slashed, chopped, and diced. And now the big confrontation is at hand and we know it's just going to be a doozy of a battle because the hero, katana clutched in his fists, has just taken the "first attack position." Or something like that.

These novels—there is probably one in your library right now and if not, you know the kind, centered around Asia and with a one-word Japanese title—are usually exciting to read and entertaining. Occasionally too, they demonstrate some research on the part of the author. But when the plot calls for characters to take up their trusty katana, too often more imagination is employed than is a reliance on reliable background sources.

The "first attack position" is a good example. It seems like every other novel of this genre describes these sorts of positions and puts the hero in one in preparation for battle. Perhaps it is because Western fencing makes use of such nomenclature, numbering various attacks and defenses. There is, however, in Japanese methods of combat, no such thing. In fact, every kendoka or any other martial artist who practices a discipline based on the use of the sword has been taught that attack and defense must be as nearly simultaneous as possible. There are no "attack" or "defense" positions *per se* in the arts of Japanese swordsmanship. Such a one-dimensional approach is antithetical to a fundamental strategic concept of martial conflict, at least in the Japanese sense of combat. *Kamae*, which is what these authors might mean, I think, when they use the word "position," refers to an attitude expressed through posture, not to some dramatic pose.

Fight scenes in these novels (and in movies and TV as well) frequently include another misconception, a bizarre one to anyone who's seen the kata of classical schools of swordsmanship. Somehow, the writers or choreographers of these tales have decided karate-like kicks are necessary as a sort of supplementary martial technique to spice up a duel with swords. I saw such a fight recently on a police show, with a couple of *yakuza* gangsters waging a battle that included acrobatic leaping kicks interspersed with the clashing of their blades. (By the way, could someone tell the sound effects guys that Japanese swords, drawn from wooden scabbards, really don't make those slithery metallic *ziiinnngg!* sounds?) These theatrics might be spectacular and keep you tuned in, but they are as phony to the knowledgeable reader as those teeth-clenching *tsuba-zeriai* where the combatants stand glare-to-glare, swords crossed and locked at the guards.

Most unarmed combative systems developed because people who needed them either did not have ready access to weapons or because for social or religious reasons, did not want to use them. Combative exponents well armed did not deliberately go about compromising their effectiveness by not using the weapon in favor of a kick or punch. Despite romantic claims to the contrary, in a fight between trained and experienced exponents, a weapon is a tremendous advantage. Only under the most extraordinary or unusual circumstances could anyone get away with kicking at a swordsman and leave the encounter as a biped. And only under the most dire and desperate of situations would a swordsman ignore his weapon's considerable value as a cutting or striking implement and resort to kicking or hitting an opponent with his arms and legs.

Related to this sort of dramatic fantasy is the literary and cinematic device of the martial arts hero tossing aside his weapon to confront his enemy empty-handed. Besides being a phenomenally stupid strategy, this is a classic example of cross-cultural confusion.

There are other inaccuracies in the paperback ryu's view of martial arts in general and in their depictions of swordplay in particular. *Katana frequently triumph over automatic firearms,* for instance. I assume most of my readers know that wouldn't happen too often in real life. *Blades cleave bodies neatly at impossible trajectories.* The reality is that, given the weight distribution and cross-section shape of a Japanese sword, clean cuts are very difficult; bloody, messy hacking is often the result. *Swordsmen don't have regular jobs but are instead living like warrior-monks in mist-shrouded dojo or plotting world domination according to the mystical precepts of bushido.* Well, of course, this is absolutely correct.

Okay, so what's my point? These *are* fiction, after all. If you want accurate information about Japanese swordsmanship, you can read scholarly texts on the subject, right? Well, there are two flaws in that argument. One, very, very few books are available in English that provide that accurate information. For every good one, there are at least a dozen that are more like fiction, full of errors, distortions, and pure fantasy. Two, the average reader of these novels rarely pursues a more scholarly look. For every reader who devours well-written factual accounts, how many more will there be who glean all their knowledge from *Shogun*?

Popular fiction plays a big part in shaping opinion and interest. Every kendoka can tell you about the guy who shows up because he's read one of these novels and wants to learn techniques like "the interlacing cross" or "returning swallow stroke." Budoka need to know that paperback novels to some degree have inspired many newcomers to the dojo. Public opinion in general about budo is influenced by these books. Less than reputable dojo have cashed in on this: look at the teachers who have hinted about their experiences battling elements of the Japanese underworld or of the murky connections they have with international law agencies. As usual, honest dojo will be explaining that the fictional martial artist and his real life counterpart are quite different. It isn't easy, or always successful, and it's too bad we're forced to fight such battles to maintain the integrity of our arts. But what else can one do, other than assume that first attack position and carry on?

I'm Sorry . . . You Okay?

I had not been training in karate for too long when Mr. Yanagi, a friend of my sensei, came for a visit. Mr. Yanagi was a gem buyer from Naha, Okinawa, when he was not practicing karate. He was an expert in pearls, and over dinner, he explained to me how pearls are cultured and how they can be "fixed" to make them look better than they are. I learned how a tincture of Merthiolate can give a substandard pearl a pinkish luster, or how pearls that have a sickly yellowish cast about them can be bleached. I was later able to use a lot of what he told me to impress girlfriends when we were visiting jewelry stores.

Yanagi-san did not look like a gem buyer. He was short and thick and powerful. At my sensei's suggestion, after dinner our visitor took me into our dojo to work with me on basics. Against my *oi-zuki* (stepping-in punch), he shifted like he was on ball bearings and countered with various techniques. We'd been at this for about an hour, gradually increasing our pace. I was still not posing any great threat to him, but Yanagi-san was having to move just a bit faster to avoid my attack. That is when he miscalculated, just fractionally. He pivoted and snapped out his fist as I moved in—and he caught me squarely on my nose with the back of his knuckles. There was no *kime*, no focus, to the blow. If there had been, my head would have come off. The strike was more just a kind of slap. But Mr. Yanagi's timing was perfect, even if there was no force behind it.

Even though he barely grazed my nose, tears squirted into my eyes. My feet and legs, still driving forward, were way ahead of the rest of me. I went down like I'd been sledgehammered. The back of my head smacked against the wooden floor. I laid there a second. I knew nothing was seriously hurt, and that I should be leaping back up quickly so as not to put myself at risk of a follow-up attack. But I wasn't sure where "up" was. All I could see were starbursts.

"*Sumimasen,*" Yanagi-san said, "*Daijobu desu ka?*" "My fault. You okay?"

I'm not sure how I expected Mr. Yanagi to react to the accident. Over the years of my training that have followed, however, I have heard that phrase many more times. I have, due to my own clumsiness and ineptitude, had occasion to use it myself. Ask anyone who has practiced with me much at all. And I have come to realize since that afternoon in the dojo, that what Yanagi-san said to me is really all one can say in a situation like that. More importantly, in the context of the budo, it is all one *should* say.

It is quite an awful feeling to hurt someone under almost any circumstances, obviously. This is especially so in the dojo where one's accidental victim is likely to be a friend or a training partner and one feels towards that person almost as if they were a brother or sister. If it is a senior that you have clobbered, you feel terrible because you've repaid the kindness of his instructing you by battering him. If it is a junior, you feel worse: a junior in the dojo is dependent upon you for his progress, not for abuse. The initial response to causing an accident in the dojo—the unconditioned response of the untrained budoka—is to abandon instantly whatever exercise it is, to rush forward, apologizing profusely and checking for damage.

The dojo, however, is not a place for unconditioned responses. The budoka who go there to practice must be willing to give a great deal of their lives over to the crafting and shaping of very highly conditioned responses. They are seeking to respond correctly to every contingency, in a wide variety of situations. Among those contingencies is the possibility of an accident. The budoka must realize there is a chance, a risk involved, every time he trains. When you allow me, for the purposes of our learning, to uncork punches at your face, or to twist your wrists to nearly the point of injury, or strike at you with a weapon, you are accepting the possibility I might miss, go a bit too far. I assume the same; that I may injure you. We have voluntarily accepted what insurance companies call "assumed risk." Like mountain climbers, big wave surfers, and ski racers, budoka would be idiots if they thought the martial Ways were risk-free. That is simply not the nature of these Ways.

If we have trained properly and we exercise care for our partner, we can (and absolutely must) cut the odds of an accident or injury. But we can never entirely eliminate risk. So when in the dojo an accident does happen, we should not be too surprised. We should not indulge in a lot of pointless blather then. We should admit it if it was our fault, and inquire if the injury is serious enough to warrant attention. If it is serious, we'd better be calling an ambulance or rendering first aid. These require coolness and a presence of mind. There is no time, and no reason to engage in excessive apologizing which, while it might make us feel better, won't do a lot of good for our injured friend.

This attitude may seem heartless. But remember. Yanagi-san's first words to me were "my fault." He accepted the blame for the accident, simply and honestly. Then he asked if I was all right, in a way that was straightforward yet not condescending, respectful of my dignity.

Simply and honestly; straightforward and respectful. This is the best way for the budoka to behave when he has been responsible for an accident in the dojo. He will also find that it is an excellent way of meeting a number of other situations as well.

Kachinuki (Old-Style Tournaments)

Things change. It is a cliché to note this, but as one grows older, the examples of it tend to occur with more and more frequency. I encountered an example of change the other day, while talking with a group of young budoka. One of them asked me when I had begun my practice of the martial arts and Ways. When I told him, he replied, "That's the year I was born." So I was feeling like a dinosaur anyway. Then, when I mentioned the once common type of martial arts tournament called *kachinuki*, all I got in response were blank stares. None of them had heard of kachinuki, none had ever participated in what was once a major social activity in the budo and a fundamental training method. It was as though I was talking to people who had never been sledding on a snowy evening or eaten caramel apples at a fair.

A few decades ago, the idea of *shiai*, or contests, in karate, judo, and kendo was quite different than it is today. The emphasis then was on an interaction between various dojo. Members got to see and experience the techniques used by others, methods taught in other schools. There was also a great deal of social interaction. Martial arts contests were almost always followed by potluck dinners and informal parties. Many budoka of non-Japanese ancestry got their first taste of sushi, sashimi, and other Japanese food after these shiai back in the sixties, made by the mothers, wives, and girlfriends of contestants. Oh, and one other thing about those shiai that distinguished them from today's matches: there were, technically speaking, no winners.

It sounds odd, a contest with no winners. But here is the way a kachinuki-type shiai worked. Beginning at the *shimoseki* (literally, the "lower side") of the tournament hall (which is called a *shiaijo*, by the way), the contestants would line up with the lowest ranks beginning at the left, all the way up to the black belts at the *joseki* ("upper side"). The matches began with the white belt at the farthest left—at the first of the line, in other words—facing the fellow on his right. Let's call them A and B. Let's say A won. B would sit back down, and the fellow on his right, C, would be next to face A. That's right, A; the guy who just fought and is still winded. But he's lucky; he wins against C too. What happens? C sits down and D jumps up to take on A. Now you're beginning to get the idea of kachinuki shiai. You stay up and fight as long as you win. Beat five guys in a row and your reward is to face the sixth. No semifinals, no double eliminations; just fight and win or lose and sit down.

At first, kachinuki may seem like a very unfair way to run an athletic contest. After all, it is a given that the guy who's just won three matches in a row is going to be exhausted. He will be facing opponents who have been sitting and are rested. Ah, but there's one little detail I haven't mentioned. Those guys waiting their turn *were* sitting, waiting their turn in the line to fight. But they were not sitting any way they liked. They were sitting formally, on their knees, legs folded with their heels on their buttocks, in the position of *seiza*. It is a manner of sitting that, unless you are very accustomed to it, can result in the entire lower half of your body becoming numb in a short time.

No warm-ups, no preparatory "on deck" announcements were part of kachinuki shiai. You knew your turn was coming up when the competitor next to you got up for his match. When your turn came, you had to deal with wobbly, tingling legs. The contestant you would be facing had just fought; he might have been winded, but he would also have had the chance to warm up and loosen his muscles. He would be relaxed and ready to go, and if an approaching opponent wasn't careful, that opponent was going to be beaten while he was still trying to stretch out his stiffness. Then too, in a large tournament, by the time the matches had worked their way down to the far end of the line, the black belts there may have been sitting virtually motionless for a couple of hours. After that time it was a struggle even to stand up. Many a senior brown belt was able to best his senior in the black belt ranks by taking advantage of his senior's having been sitting so long he had trouble just getting to his feet, never mind making a good account of himself in competition.

So, do you see why there were no "winners" in kachinuki competition as we usually think of them? Yes, you may have beaten contestant G, but you were only able to do it after he'd fought and beaten contestants C, D, E, and F, for example. This system made categories like winners and losers mostly meaningless. Egos bloated by championships never had a chance to blossom. Trophies, if given at all, were usually awarded to the dojo which had collectively won the most matches or more likely, to those competitors who showed the best (though not always the winning) spirit.

I do not wish to paint a rosy "everyone just got together and had fun" picture of kachinuki shiai. Contestants fought. Hard. It was my experience that ten minutes after the medals were given out everyone had already forgotten who had received them, true. But we knew who had demonstrated the best technique, who we wanted to face the next time. We also remembered the techniques we saw, the wonderful displays of courage and determination, and the comradeship of the whole event.

I suppose some might continue to insist that a kachinuki-style shiai is unfair. There is not much good argument against that position. Kachinuki shiai *is* unfair, no doubt about it. It is unfair in the same sense battlefield combat is unfair, or that a real-life self-defense situation is unfair. There are no warm-ups under those circumstances either, or resting periods. Kachinuki shiai is unfair. Which is, as those of us fortunate enough to experience it have learned, a pretty good way to train for the unfairness of much of the rest of life.

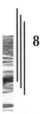

8

Uke-Waza (The Art of Taking It)

Anyone whose budo practice partners have included Hawaiians soon learns, as I did, the importance of "talk story." At the university judo club where I began my judo training, some of the members were from Hawaii. Since I was still in high school, these college boys and girls were like older brothers and sisters to me, and I always felt privileged to sit in and listen to their "talk story," a pidgin Hawaiian phrase to describe what elsewhere might be called "bull sessions." Most evenings, after judo practice was done, we would gather on the mats and discuss everything from politics to great meals to—these being university students, after all—sex. The talk story often centered around the budo. That's what we were discussing one night. Specifically, the topic was about the toughest individuals we had each encountered. One of the group told of another judoka he had trained with in Japan, a Japanese champion who had thrown opponents so hard that even using proper breakfalls, they were knocked unconscious by the force of hitting the mat. Another recounted the abilities of a Chinese martial artist he'd met who could employ vicious footsweeps that literally somersaulted his opponents. These stories went on and on. One fellow said the toughest people he'd ever met were Special Forces personnel in Vietnam; another insisted it was the British SAS teams.

It was Clyde Kimura, from Kauai, who spoke with a kind of final authority on the subject. The toughest individuals he had ever encountered, he said, were kendoka. "The old ones," he said. "A kendo man who's in his mid-sixties; been training about 50 years," Kimura said firmly, "he can take an incredible amount of abuse."

I have often reflected on Kimura-san's words. Interesting, isn't it, that his concept of toughness was not in how much one can dish out, but how much one can take?

Many of the karate masters from the old days made a great deal of the importance of *uke-waza*. The word is usually translated as "blocking techniques." Actually, it means "techniques of 'receiving.'" Recently, the senior JKA instructor in Great Britain, Keinosuke Enoeda, criticized the stagnant and limited techniques he saw in karate competition. An improvement, he advised, would be to "practice hard to acquire a profound knowledge of the unique uke-waza of karate." Enoeda sensei's advice will sound strange to the average karate exponent, especially to those tournament enthusiasts who are always advocating just the opposite strategy for winning karate contests. They focus their practice on more varied and dramatic strikes. But Enoeda went on to explain his reasoning. "Once you are confident in *ukeru* [receiving] you can anticipate any attack. It is important to attack properly with full confidence and vigor however hard you are pushed. Using this offensive ukeru, you can undermine your opponent and gain a winning chance."

What Enoeda sensei was saying is not easy to understand. It requires some thought, and more. The karateka who wants to grasp Enoeda's advice must be prepared to put some time in on the dojo floor, thinking about this advice with his body. "Unique uke-waza" tells us that karate's receiving methods may be special to karate. "Offensive uke" hints that there might be something more to uke-waza than just passively anticipating an attack and then responding. True mastery of uke is the ability to deal with any kind of attack, at any *stage* of the attack. The adept of uke-waza has a feel for what shape his opponent's strike will take, from what angle and so on. He can nullify it or let it come, already prepared for an appropriate counter. This approach to karate is only one half of a complete strategy. The other half is *kakari-waza*, or "attacking methods." But no matter how strong one develops his kakari-waza, he must always work to polish his receiving techniques. This is a skill absolutely essential to karate competition, where one must cope with all sorts of spirited attacks.

Back in the sixties, one of the great competitors in Japanese karate was Tetsuhiko Asai, of the Japan Karate Association. One of Asai's favorite techniques was to charge right at the front kick of an opponent. As the kicking leg extended, Asai would duck underneath, coming up behind his attacker and countering. It was a remarkable demonstration of uke-waza. (And not always successful; Asai lost an eye when he misjudged a kick once.) Asai had to be able to ascertain instantly and exactly the depth and level the kick was coming at, to "receive" it effectively. Uke-waza, performed at this level, is a different way of looking at toughness. It means being able to "take it" and to respond appropriately.

As I said, uke-waza is combined with kakari-waza, attacking techniques, to form a complete strategy. They must be balanced. It is easier to study and refine one's attacking skills. Uke-waza takes more patience. Both, however, are necessary. Strengthening your attacks while neglecting uke-waza will result in a strategy that can be compromised or defeated when confronting an opponent who is stronger or more cunning and can get around your attack. Practice uke-waza exclusively and you will find yourself unable to initiate or to lead. You will always be responding and unnaturally passive. Learn to use and manipulate them both and you will begin to see what balance in the budo is all about . . . and the potential of its applications far beyond the confines of the training hall.

9

Death of a Warrior

When Noritsune
Drowned himself
Three trails of bubbles rose.

This has always been among my favorite *senryu*, one of the pithy verses of Japanese poetry, rather like the more familiar haiku, which are often keen observations on the human condition. This brief senryu, in three short lines, has much to say about the fighting spirit of the warrior.

Noritsune Noto no kami was a general of the great clan of the Taira, a warrior family bent on the control of the entire country of Japan. In the spring of 1185, the Taira were at the long end of a century-old war with Japan's other most prominent samurai clan, the Minamoto. Led by Minamoto Yoritomo and his brother Yoshitsune, the Minamoto had dogged the forces of the Taira clan all over southern Japan. They followed the Taira finally into the latter's stronghold, on the southern island of Shikoku. In a daring attack at dawn, Yoshitsune led a flotilla of boats into the harbor of the town where the Taira were gathered, wreaking havoc, putting most of the town to the torch. The Taira fled to their own ships; a fierce and climactic battle in the struggle between the two clans erupted in the straits of the sea at Dan-o-ura. It would decide for all time which clan would emerge as the most powerful.

Noritsune's skill as a tactician was legendary, as was his ability in personal combat. He had never lost a battle in which he commanded troops. He was a master archer and an expert with the *naginata*. In the earlier encounter with the Minamoto, Noritsune had boldly charged, by himself, right up to the enemy lines when he spotted his archrival Yoshitsune in an exposed position. Yoshitsune's retainers saw Noritsune coming. Quickly, they insinuated themselves between him and their leader. In spite of this human shield, Noritsune, wielding his famous Shigeto bow, fired arrows fletched with hawk feathers at his enemy, dropping eight of the Minamoto samurai surrounding Yoshitsune. One of his targets was pierced from the left shoulder to the right side.

In the final sea battle at Dan-o-ura, Noritsune was a demon. He boarded a Minamoto boat and laid waste to several of the enemy with his long-handled naginata. On the rocking, pitching boats, hand-to-hand combat was breaking out. In the confusion, it was some time before Noritsune caught sight of Yoshitsune. As soon as he did, he charged. But Yoshitsune, who had learned his own martial skills, legend had it, from mountain goblins called *tengu*, employed a method of jumping in armor that allowed him to leap successfully to another boat. Within the time it took the oarsmen to pull half a dozen strokes, Yoshitsune had once again escaped.

Enraged at the loss of another opportunity to kill Yoshitsune, Noritsune tore off all his armor except for his breastplate, one woven with fine Chinese silk. He shouted to the boats of his enemy, the Minamoto, rocking all around him. "Isn't there a single warrior among you who wishes to take me on?"

Aki-no-Taro Sanemoto, a Minamoto samurai who was an expert in grappling, took up the challenge. He, his brother Jiro, and another Minamoto retainer launched a small dory-like boat toward the larger vessel where Noritsune waited. They leaped aboard and attacked as a group. With a kick, Noritsune knocked one retainer into the drink. He seized Aki-no-Taro in a wristlock, then grabbed Jiro. "Come on," he roared, "let's climb the Mountain of Death!" And with his enemies in tow, he jumped into the foaming swells of the straits.

Three trails of bubbles rose . . .

Noritsune's sacrifice, like most of the famous sacrifices of the samurai throughout their history, is remembered principally because it was futile. The Taira lost. They lost the battle at Dan-o-ura, and shortly thereafter, they lost the war with the Minamoto entirely. Their clan was doomed. But the spirit of Noritsune is a perfect example of the fighting spirit of the samurai at its best. The violence of combat as it is popularly depicted in modern movies or other forms of fiction tends to be horribly fraudulent. Popular heroes in these take on a whole army of enemies it seems, tackling a regiment of terrorists or a battalion of gangsters or the majority of the adult male population of any country in Southeast Asia. And while our hero may be bloodied a bit or bruised—and his shirt will always be torn—we may be sure that by the time the credits are rolling or the final page has been turned, he will have emerged the victor.

Those of us fortunate enough to have been exposed to the tales of the campaigns between the Taira and the Minamoto when we were kids learned a valuable lesson. We learned that heroes don't always win. Sometimes, as with Noritsune, they die. They go down, taking as many of the enemy with them as they can—that's part of what makes them heroes. But they die, nonetheless. In a battle against overwhelming odds, victory is not always possible. But here is the lesson for the warrior: going into a battle with the spirit of Noritsune, with the determination to die and take as many opponents with you as you can, does not guarantee success or victory. You will not always win. Yet with that kind of spirit, can it ever be truly said of you that you lost?

10

The Dead Zone

Choose a stance, one from the repertoire of karate, or judo, or aikido; any of the budo. Get set in it; really get yourself as solid as you can be. Then have a dojomate give you a little push. Just a gentle shove. Chances are, if your training's been good you'll be able to withstand the push. That's one purpose of a strong stance. But have him continue to give pushes and as he does, have him move around you slowly, pushing from different angles as he circles your stance. There is no need for him to hurry or to try to sneak a quick push in when you don't expect it. At some point in this exercise, your friend is going to topple your balance. He has found your *shikaku*, your "dead zone."

Some budoka might doubt their balance can be upset, particularly when they are prepared for an attempt to do it, particularly when the push isn't going to be a surprise, particularly among those who have come to believe their stances are immovable. But try it somewhere in the radius of pushes, even a very moderate force will break down your stance. Don't worry. Your failure to maintain your balance has nothing to do with any flaws in your practice or in the stance. It has to do with the shikaku that is inherent in any stance and in any human's posture.

At its most basic level, shikaku maybe thought of as the angle (or angles, to be more exact) where an upright human is vulnerable in terms of balance. It is, in a kinesiological sense, his blind side. In a left front stance as one might take in karate, your partner can slam his sweeping left foot against your left foot all day long in a lateral motion, to no avail. But if he hooks his foot slightly and sweeps at a shallow angle to his right rear corner, you'll go down like you have been hit with a cattle prod. In that stance, that direction, your own left front, is the angle of your shikaku. In aikido against a wrist grab you rotate your seized hand as if you were going to strike your attacker in his face with your *tegatana,* or "hand sword." Doing so causes his upper body to twist away. You are able to pin his arm in the basic aikido technique of *ikkyo*. But it isn't until the aikidoka learns to shift his body center slightly at the onset, to readjust his extension of power against the opponent's dead zone, that ikkyo and every other aikido technique really work.

As you have probably discovered by my descriptions so far, shikaku is a difficult concept of the budo to describe. Too often, exponents have only a fragmented view of shikaku, and so they are not able to exploit it fully in an opponent or minimalize its effects in themselves. The stance experiment described above is illustrative of just a small facet of shikaku, for example. Against a stable, stationary position (such as a stance), it is possible for even an unskilled person to find another's shikaku. Rotate 360° around him, pushing at every angle of the circle and you'll eventually strike it. That, however, is a controlled experiment, where there is no moving resistance. Try finding the shikaku against someone who is moving, shifting his balance point constantly along with his stances, closing and lengthening his distance from you (and trying to find *your* shikaku as well). That is shikaku in real life.

Since, except for very good meditation disciples and your average dedicated couch potato, we tend to be mobile in our waking lives, our shikaku are mobile, too. The angles of vulnerability in our posture are in constant flux and flow and just as importantly, they are multidimensional. This latter can be observed when the tai chi expert seems to pull in a partner in "pushing hands," drawing him forward and down and then shooting him up and back, uprooting his stance dramatically. In karate, a properly executed rising block takes advantage of an attacker's dead zone, up and to the rear of the attacker's punching arm.

Perhaps the best-known illustration of shikaku is a portrait of the eccentric swordsman Miyamoto Musashi. Gripping both his long and short swords, Musashi's posture and countenance are electric with power. His slit-eyed stare is furious; wholly concentrated. Any number of his biographers and interpreters of Musashi's writings have suggested there is some meaning in the posture of the warrior in this remarkable portrait. Most of these interpretations are drawn from the discipline of kendo, an art incidentally, that Musashi never practiced. I would, rather presumptuously, like to add my own thoughts about that painting.

To me, Musashi's portrait is like some kind of *koan*, one of the mental/spiritual quandaries posed to disciples of Zen by their masters. It is a simple rendering. Musashi stands erect, dressed plainly in kimono and a *haori* vest, and his swords, long and short, are gripped in a position that does not seem very martial or threatening at all. They appear to droop in front of him. The expression on his face is, as I said, fiercely concentrated. But it does not seem to be directed at any outer enemy. It is enigmatic; fascinating the more you look at it. Musashi seems to be locked in a profound internal struggle of sorts. Perhaps it is only my imaginative interpretation, but when I contemplate his famous portrait, I see a man struggling with what must have been for someone in his profession, a fundamental obstacle. Musashi stands alone, utterly absorbed, seeking a way to overcome the limitations of shikaku. Think of it. No matter how he stands or holds the sword—even to the extent of taking one for each hand—he must still contend with the dead zone. He must still acknowledge that, as a human, like all humans, he can never be completely invulnerable. From a purely technical point of view, from the perspective of combat strategy, this must have been a psychological monkey clinging to the back of every professional warrior like Musashi. Whatever kamae (combative posture or attitude) they assumed, there was always the shikaku. There was a weakness to every stance, to every position of holding the sword.

Moreover, Musashi was not merely another swordsman. He was as well an artist, a philosopher. And so I wonder if Musashi was contemplating, in this stern-eyed portrait, not just the shikaku he faced in combat but the vulnerabilities he faced in life. Was he considering the unexpected angle of attack of an enemy's sword? Or the surprise assaults to which all of us are susceptible: illness, heartbreak, loneliness, death? "How would you respond to this attack?" one of my sensei asked me when he was teaching me one morning, and he grabbed my wrist. I performed a pivot and locked his wrist, using the grip against him. "And this one?" He punched and I countered, punching back, turning his strike aside with my blow and stopping my fist on the spot just to the side of his chin where it would cause the most nerve damage if it connected. He paused and looked at me. "And how about this attack?" he asked. "How about if you have a child someday," he said, "and the doctors tell you he has an incurable case of childhood cancer. How would you handle *that* attack?"

I wonder if, in devoting most of his life to overcoming the limitations of shikaku in the art of the sword, Musashi had not entered into a struggle as well on a different plane. I wonder if his training in the martial arts eventually led to a deeper understanding of the shikaku of life. The possibility that it might, in my opinion, is reason enough to head off for the dojo for still another training session.

11

Counting to a Thousand

This was the question: "Is there anything more irritating than a person who has dabbled a year or so in this art, a year or two in another and who then thinks himself an all-around competent martial artist?" It was posed conversationally by one of my seniors at the dojo, to another budoka, also far my senior.

"Yes," the second replied, "there is. It is the fellow who has trained several years in one art, who then thinks of himself as an all-around competent martial artist."

I never forgot that exchange, probably because I have had several occasions in my budo practice since to observe examples of it. Once, for instance, I saw a karateka, very good, at the third level of black belt *(sandan)*, engaging in an intense free exchange of technique with another karateka of similar skill with a level of grading at *yondan*, one rank higher. These kinds of exchanges, at these levels of ability, tend to be just a few degrees short of an actual fight. The action was swift and powerful. The sandan slid forward and shifted his weight to his rear leg. He started to lift his front foot for a kick, then changed his mind. But before he could regain balance, his opponent unleashed a vicious sweep that got both sandan's legs. His body flew up in a wide arc. He was airborne, fully horizontal to the ground. With my background in judo, I expected him to take the simple fall easily. He didn't. He tumbled and sprawled clumsily and dislocated a wrist. He was a third *dan* in karate and he'd never taken the time to train at a judo or aikido school to learn falling techniques.

Another time I saw an aikido teacher snatch punches right and left from attacking students, converting them into wrist reversals that ended in spectacular throws. The attackers flew all over the dojo, until the teacher ill-advisedly encouraged, "Come on, *very* strong strikes," and the next aikidoka coming at him was also a karateka with a front punch that connected faster than lightning and packed only slightly less wallop. The aikido sensei did not get up for a while.

Speaking of aikido, how many times have you seen demonstrations where an aikidoka plucks a *bokken*, a wooden practice sword, away from an opponent in mid-strike with one of aikido's *tachi-dori* or "sword-taking" techniques? They are almost mesmerizing. Would you like to see him try that against a Japanese collegiate kendo champion? Me too. Then I'd like to see that kendo champ try his stuff against an exponent of the classical *koryu*, the traditional art of using the sword on the battlefield. (As a matter of fact, I have seen the latter, more than once, and the kendoka escaped dismemberment only because the koryu fencer's blades were oak instead of steel.)

The point here is not one-upmanship. Precisely the opposite. The point is, a single martial Way is certainly sufficiently broad and deep enough for he who follows it to gain harmony with the universe, to lead a worthwhile life, to accomplish, in short, all of those most noble of goals that should motivate the serious martial artist. But no form of the Japanese budo, no martial discipline in the world is "complete" in a combative sense of that word. That is because fighting systems developed as the results of specific needs. The Japanese warrior's *koryu bujutsu* (traditional battlefield martial arts), for instance, and the Indonesian farmer's combative methods of *silat* are both arts of fighting. But that is about all they have in common. The weapons, strategies, footwork, training regimens, and so on, are all much more different than they are similar. The samurai developed his arts to use on the battleground. He was employing them against other professional warriors. The Indonesian farmer (and later the nobility who refined it) evolved their art of silat as more a means of civilian self-defense. Both arts are an intrinsic part of their native cultures. Neither of them—nor any other fighting art—has a monopoly on effectiveness.

This may seem discouraging, to learn that no one art is going to answer all your combative or self-defense needs. But it shouldn't. Rather, we should celebrate this as an example of mankind's endless ingenuity and resourcefulness. Each art has its own flavors, its own specialties, and yes, its own inherent weaknesses. We should also—and this too, is the point—take advantage of the fact we live in the 20th century. Unlike the samurai or the silat practitioner, we have available to us instruction in fighting arts from all over Asia. Why not exploit this opportunity?

I am not, as some may think, advocating an "If it's Thursday this must be tai chi night" approach of smorgasbord training. But I do think that once one has grasped the essentials of one art (a process that takes, at least with the Japanese budo, a good ten years), he ought to look around. He ought to at least observe the training of other disciplines. And perhaps he ought to give them a try to see how what he has learned compares and contrasts. In so doing, he's bound to learn something, even if it is only that he likes his original Way best. At least his opinion will have been formed by experience and not by the narrow-mindedness of "my art is the ultimate" that characterizes so much of the attitudes to be found in the fighting arts these days.

There is a saying among students of the calligraphic brush that, while it is important to master the single horizontal stroke for the character of "one," it is impossible to count to a thousand without learning other strokes, other characters. Learn the basics, and learn them well. But do not believe you have mastered the art of writing to a thousand because your character "one" is perfect.

12

Jaku (Tranquillity)

I always felt fortunate to have been the only student of my sensei. True, it meant I didn't have any other students around to help with chores, but it also meant I enjoyed the privilege of having all my teacher's attention. There were, though, occasional inquiries from other people who wanted to train in the art of swordsmanship with him. Most of them he put off without much trouble. A few were persistent. I remember a fellow who made several trips of well over one hundred miles, coming to watch us train and asking Sensei if he might be taken on as a student. He gave every indication he was going to keep this up. Since we trained outside, Sensei started to worry that the guy might stand around watching us and end up freezing to death since winter was on its way.

I suspect too, that my teacher really wasn't interested in another student. I was enough of a pain in the backside to him. But he finally agreed he'd teach the fellow, provided the guy met one qualification. Sensei knew of a teacher of the tea ceremony who lived in this guy's town. Spend a year studying the tea ceremony, he told the guy, and I'll teach you the sword. The guy was surprised, as you can imagine, and asked why. "If you're tough enough to last a year of chado (tea ceremony)," said Sensei, "then swordsmanship won't be much of a problem."

We never saw the guy after that. My guess is he found Sensei a bit too eccentric, the "qualification" too odd. But my hope is he actually began training in chado and became so engrossed he followed it exclusively.

Readers might find my teacher's qualification odd, too. It isn't really. Once the *chajin* (tea ceremony student) has taken up a martial art, and once a *bugeisha* (martial artist) has given chado a serious effort, the relationship between the spirit of the two becomes clear to both.

Now look: I'm not saying learning to make a bowl of tea will make you a master swordsman. That old story about the tea master who had to fight the samurai and so went into the duel with a "tea mind" is a nice tale. But spirit, no matter how strong, can never replace technical ability. You want to learn to use a sword, study swordsmanship. Don't think you're going to learn the skills of a martial art through tea or flower arranging. It isn't magic. Even so, there's a fascinating overlap in the training and in the mentality of both.

Sensei liked to perform a kind of tea ceremony done outside, at the doorway of a rickety, abandoned barn that stood—but just barely—out in the countryside near where we used to sometimes practice with the sword. He thought the weathered grey boards and the angles of shadow and light formed by the wide doorway were a perfect background for chado, and the view, overlooking some hills, was peaceful as well. So I carried the equipment up from where we parked, and after Sensei made a charcoal fire in the brazier, we'd go down to the open pasture below the barn with our bokken and train.

My winter practice uniform consisted of the heaviest weight *judogi*-type jacket and pants along with a heavy cotton *hakama*. I'd also wear a long-sleeved undershirt called a *hadagi*. Layered like that I'd usually keep warm in all but the coldest weather, as much because of the clothes as because the energy exerted in practice was enough to heat me up. But on this particular day, dark, pewter-colored clouds pushed across the sky, and just as we were finishing going through all the kata, they let loose their load of snow. By the time we'd finished and walked back up to the old barn, my head and shoulders were dusted with white. I was already shivering. Because of the snowfall, I assumed Sensei would cancel our tea ceremony. No such luck.

The *nodate* or outside form of the ceremony calls for the host to wipe clean the tea equipment, rinse the bowl, then prepare the tea, all with precise, controlled movements that are executed with the same spirit and self-discipline of the kata of the martial arts. Since my sensei was taking the part of the host, my role was that of the guest. I had to sit quietly, observing him, and then accept and drink the bowl of tea he offered.

While the barn's eaves protected us from some of the falling snow, each little gust of wind would send in a generous sprinkling. Soon, as I was sitting kneeling, I had tiny rows of snow collecting in the pleats of my hakama. We were sitting on *mushiro*, a kind of rice straw matting that is much like the kind you take to the beach. They're not thick; it wasn't long before the cold of the dirt floor crept through. My teeth chattered. My hands, held together in my lap, were getting pale and they throbbed with the cold. My whole body shivered and spasmed.

Curiously, however, the more miserable I became, the more comfortable my sensei appeared to be. He busied himself, wiping the tea scoop with a small cloth and rinsing the bowl, and I realized my hands were so numb I'd probably have a tough time holding that bowl when he handed it to me. Sensei did not shiver, did not hurry. He was taken completely with the kata of making tea. His movements were no different than they'd have been if we were in a cozy teahouse in summer rather than in the doorway of a tottering old barn in the middle of what was rapidly becoming a snowstorm.

When he finally set the steaming tea bowl in front of me, I bowed stiffly and took it with wooden, clumsy fingers that ached for the warmth that came through the ceramic. One doesn't just take up the bowl and slurp it off, though. Instead, I had to display some sort of composure, admiring the beauty of the bowl, the rich, emerald color of the tea. And so I had to wait, to contemplate, to sip slowly and to reach inside myself to try to find the same kind of calmness I tried to find when I was facing Sensei with a bokken in my hand rather than a tea bowl.

Sensei let his gaze drift out to where the lower end of the pasture was lost in the swirl of white. "One time the tea master Sen no Rikyu was asked about the secret of mastering tea," he said. Then he looked at me. "His answer was 'Cool in summer; warm in winter.' That's interesting, don't you think?"

"*Oshimai wo*," I said at last, returning the empty bowl to Sensei. "I am finished." But in understanding the Ways of tea and the sword, I wasn't finished. Not by any means. I am only just beginning.

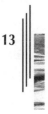

13

Kata and Boeuf Bourguignon

Do you know of Paul Bocuse? Think of him as the Gichin Funakoshi of modern French cuisine. Bocuse, a culinary genius, has reinvented classic French cooking in many fundamental ways. His Paris restaurant is like a Mecca for those who adore great food. His books and lectures have made him a celebrity the world over. A few years ago, Bocuse expanded his empire by opening cooking schools in different cities. One of them was in Osaka. As you may know if you've watched the TV program *Iron Chef*, French food is wildly popular in all Japan. One of the most incongruous sights of my life was in a little village outside Nara. There were not more than half a dozen shops here, a noodle restaurant, a bamboo supplier—and right in the middle, a French-style patisserie.

Bocuse was brought to Japan to give a cooking course in his Osaka culinary academy. The lesson for the day: boeuf bourguignon, a rich, stewed beef with vegetables and a luscious, thick gravy. Bocuse was preparing this classic of Burgundian cuisine while hundreds of apprentice chefs looked on with rapt attention, taking notes. As he put the dish together, he adapted. He added chunks of beef, then scattered in a fistful of onions, eyeing the pot as he did to make sure he was getting all in balance. A student interrupted his work. "Sensei," the student said, "that's not how the dish is prepared."

Bocuse is a brilliant chef, a master at his trade. But he has a typical Gallic impatience with interruptions, an even more typical French disdain for the impertinence of those who would question his genius. It is hard to imagine Bocuse not heaving the contents of the pot at the questioner. He did not, though, and undeterred, the student plunged ahead. "Escoffier's book clearly says that for one kilogram of beef, you have to add 250 grams of onions and 100 milligrams of salt."

Amazingly, Bocuse did not explode. He responded patiently. "Okay," he said through his interpreter. "Instead of making beef bourguignon, let's paint. Let's all paint a picture of a rose. I will give all of you the tubes of paint, red, white, green. There are 400 of you in here today. Do you believe all 400 of your pictures will look exactly the same?"

The point of his lesson is illustrative; that it should be made to an audience of Japanese is, from the perspective of us budoka at any rate, more than a little pertinent.

What is the most persistent criticism of kata made by those not actually engaged in a serious, long-term study of it? They are robotic, right? They are, the critics insist, a pointless attempt to jam some sort of orthodoxy into the context of combat, a misguided effort at making spontaneous reality (which is a real fight) into a rehearsed, choreographic encounter. Kick A must follow Punch 3; the former executed *exactly* at 90° from the direction of the latter. On and on.

The truthful response to this criticism is that kata, as it is practiced in modern karate, is a means of instilling certain behaviors, some reactive, some proactive. Kata does not provide the "story" of a fight, it is rather the grammar that allows us to tell our own stories, as varied as are the encounters one is likely to meet, with fluidity and a coherent structure that is likely to win us the battle. We *say* that. But we need, from time to time, to pause and consider if it is really so. Too many karateka, in their kata training, get caught up in exactly those habits for which their art is criticized. Like the apprentice chefs under Bocuse's instruction, they run to the book or to the teacher to make sure what they are doing is exactly, precisely as it has been laid out.

Nothing wrong with this. Up to a point. It is one of the great strengths of karate that we have kata which can be depended upon. But if we stop at that stage of training, concentrate *only* on the exact replication of the kata, we lose part of the kata's inherent value. For a few years now, many of the top karate sensei in Japan have been moving away from this very stultified perspective of kata as a series of movements the details of which are carved in stone. They have been urging more advanced karateka to go beyond the perfection of the preset form and begin exploring the potential contained within the kata. The JKA's Tetsuhiko Asai is at the front of this. He has used the analogy of writing. Block printing is the child's introduction to writing, Asai says. Later, the child adds the more free-flowing cursive letters. Finally, he develops a unique hand that is so individual it can be used as a means of identifying the writer. Our karate, Asai and others are saying, needs to develop the same way.

Certainly we cannot get to our own, unique "interpretation" of writing without going through the stages of learning to print and then to write in cursive strokes. Likewise, we cannot go into the dojo and "riff" on a kata, pulling out this and that and adapting it in a distinctive way. Not without really, deeply understanding that kata first. We must submit ourselves to the rigors of learning it exactly as it is taught. To return to our original analogy, I doubt Paul Bocuse's personal take on boeuf bourguignon would taste as delicious as it does had he not done a lot of time pouring over Escoffier's book himself. Learning to make it exactly as the master wrote. But we cannot be satisfied with mastering the form and leaving it at that. We have to aim beyond.

It is a narrow road to walk. If we start extemporizing too soon, before we truly understand the fundamentals of kata, we are wasting our time. If we continue, year after year, to just copy, never thinking of our individual take on these same kata, we are spinning our wheels as well. This is a constant challenge for the karateka, to find the balance and to keep it, throughout the whole of his journey on this Way.

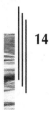

14

Barefoot

Why do we go barefoot while practicing karate and other forms of the budo?

It is not a question to keep philosophers restless and tossing in their beds, admittedly. Nor, in comparison with many of the truly serious problems the budo face, is it a question that ought to deeply concern those of us who follow the martial Ways. But are you, like me, wondering every time you see someone in a karate *keikogi* with a pair of shoes on his feet, "What's wrong with this picture?"

Karate is traditionally practiced, as are all Japanese budo, *hadashi*—barefoot. Some of the reasons for this are cultural. In Japan, where footwear is not worn indoors, shoes never developed as a part of normal clothing as they did in the West. The Japanese have for centuries worn *geta*, thonged wooden clogs when walking outdoors. They also developed *zori* (like modern beach "flip-flops"). Both these kinds of footgear could be slipped on and off easily while going from inside a house to the outside. Then too, like any feudal agricultural society where the climate permitted it, the peasant class in Japan most often went barefoot. The houses and other buildings they used, then and now, were floored with tatami mats or smooth wooden planks. Both surfaces would have been quickly damaged by almost any kind of shoe.

This custom has had some interesting influences on the development of Japanese culture and civilization. The Japanese have come to distinguish clearly, in most cases, the differences between "inside" and "outside" the home. The inner parts of the house itself are reserved almost entirely for family members and very close acquaintances. Everyone else is kept at a certain distance. There are some exceptions to this; particularly in rural areas, the *doma,* or earthen-floored kitchen area was kind of an in-between place separating the inner house from the outside. But this approach to architecture and to daily living has meant that in many cases, being barefoot or clad only in socks signifies one is in a fairly intimate setting. It is, in some ways, not unlike the rural lifestyle in America where visitors are welcomed by the invitation to "take your shoes off and sit a spell."

There are, however, reasons for bare feet in budo training other than in preventing damage to a floor. The most important one has to do with the physics of these arts. The delivery of power in karate, whether punching, kicking, striking, or parrying, comes off the back foot. Similarly, in kendo, to give a strike the correct focus and force, the back heel must be firmly planted. In aikido, the same is true. There can be no power in an aikido throw or pin without a strong connection to the floor through the feet. Energy is transmitted in all these budo through the solid base supplied by the feet, all through the body, to the target. (That's why karate exponents especially avoid practicing on solid concrete or tile floors; the force they're trying to generate with strong stances is ricocheted back into their bodies by an unyielding floor.) Consistent practice on this kind of unyielding surface will soon cause lower back problems and other musculoskeletal complaints. The karateka, like all budoka, needs to feel how his feet make contact with the floor in order to learn how it is he can generate power.

Movement in the budo, balanced, coordinated movement, depends in a very large way upon another part of the feet: the toes. Budoka do not push off their heels to move forward as most people walking normally do. Instead, they squeeze, starting with the toes on up through the muscles of the inner leg. The front foot draws the back one up, in a motion very similar to the pulling stride a sprinter makes when coming off the blocks. And just as the sprinter uses spikes to grip the ground, the budoka grips the floor to pull himself into his attack or block. It may take a couple of years to develop this skill even at a basic level, but it is absolutely fundamental to karate, as well as all other Japanese martial Ways. Squeeze and grip the floor with the toes; deliver power through a solid connection of the heels. Both these essentials are impossible to learn or to practice wearing shoes.

(I must note here that while all modern forms of the budo encourage this kind of footwork, the classical *bujutsu*, the martial arts of old Japan do not all conform to a single way of moving. Some of these feudal era schools teach methods of walking where the heel lands first and then the length of the foot is rolled forward in a continuous motion. Their reasoning has to do with the difficulties the samurai might have had to contend with in fighting. Battlefields were likely to be littered with bodies, broken weapons, and other debris. So a classical bujutsu would take this into account, teaching alternative methods of movement that would be efficacious under those circumstances. The modern budo have been meant to be performed on smooth, even surfaces. Their ways of movement reflect this.)

Still another reason for conducting one's budo practice without shoes has to do with some more subtle benefits that may accrue. On the bottom of the foot is located an important point along the meridians recognized by the study of acupuncture. This point, called *yungchuan* in Chinese, is actively massaged during budo practice. If you want to find the point exactly, sit down and bend your leg until you can see the bottom of your foot. Now, curl all your toes forward. You will see a slight depression form, a cavity right behind the ball of your foot, at the top of the arch. That is the point, and that is the spot too, where, when you are correctly balanced in any budo stance, your weight will be exactly centered. Some budoka make a habit of massaging this point on both feet when they wake up in the morning. Next time you are at the dojo, take a stance, then concentrate on this part of your foot. If your toes are gripping the floor and your weight distribution is correct, you will see that the yungchuan point is being stimulated.

All this does not preclude training in shoes entirely. Experienced karateka ought to practice their techniques in shoes often enough to grasp the very different "feel" they have performing that way; outside, on varying surfaces. Even aikidoka and judoka, if they can find a suitable surface outside for taking falls, will find it useful to practice with shoes on, although they must exercise caution. If you want to practice as they occasionally did in the old days, you can try your kata or other techniques on varied terrain in geta or zori. Shoes are probably a necessity at outdoor *gasshuku* training camps that involve aerobic runs over rough ground, or in extremely cold weather when outdoor training may include the threat of frostbite. (In these instances, though, I would encourage budoka to try *jikka tabi*. These are canvas moccasins, with soft rubber soles and a split toe, worn all over Japan by farmers and construction workers. Jikka tabi will protect your feet from the cold or from rough ground while still allowing you to feel the ground and to move properly.)

"We train in the park or some other outdoor location where there is apt to be glass, sticks, rocks," goes one argument against barefoot training. Okay. Leave your shoes at home and bring a trash bag with you instead. Clean up what amounts to your dojo so the ground will be safe to train on there.

There's a place for shoes in every well-appointed martial art training hall. It's a shelved cupboard or a space on the floor where they can be taken off and left until practice is over. Go barefoot. You'll look more like a part of the tradition of the budo, and you will benefit enormously by performing karate with the correct application of footwork. And given the price of athletic shoes today, you can use the money you save on a new pair of footwear to buy your teacher a new sportscar.

15

Asobi Ja Nai . . . (Don't Play Around)

Among those of us young and not infrequently spirited boys who comprised the *shonen* (youth) division of Midwestern judo years ago, Nishimoto osho was regarded as a reincarnation of Fudo Myo-o. Fudo is the wrathful Buddhist deity who wields a sword and rope with which to terrify those who stray from the path of righteousness, and we thought Nishimoto osho looked just like him. Osho is a word for a priest, which was Nishimoto's calling. But he was also a powerful fifth dan in judo who had appointed himself our taskmaster. At every judo competition he was there, serving as an official at our matches. His discipline was granite. He believed the budo were a Way of life, to be approached with the utmost seriousness. At one tournament Nishimoto was officiating a match where Garry Matsukawa faced a much less skillful opponent. Because of that, Garry wasn't going all out. Halfway through the match he tried an unusual scissoring reap of his opponent's legs. It's called *kani basami* or "crab pincer." (Older readers will know just how long ago this was; the throw was outlawed in judo competition a long time ago.) Garry would never have tried such a risky move against someone closer to his skill level since it required him to balance on one arm, using both legs to scissor his opponent at the knees and waist.

"*Hansoku make!*" the osho shouted. Garry was disqualified. The call signified he'd violated the rules of competition. Garry was obviously mystified, as we all were. He'd broken no rules. He'd only made a playful attempt to try an odd throw. But in those days one didn't question a senior, especially not an official. *Especially* not the osho. So it was over. But later, in the dressing room, Nishimoto walked up to Garry and offered this simple explanation: *"Asobi ja nai."*

Asobi ja nai—"Don't play around." A long time's passed since that competition, and still I remember that incident. I recall it every time I hear expressions like "karate player" or "I played judo last night." I dislike those terms and I think the osho would, too. When we talk about "play"—*asobi* in Japanese—we refer to those activities engaged in for fun or recreation. Play is distinguished by its occurrence outside of daily life, and by the fact it is temporary. Aside from athletes and public servants, no one plays his whole life. Likewise, although we often believe play can teach us to get along with others, let's face it; most of us do not participate in an afternoon of Frisbee or softball in order to inculcate profound truths.

The budoka, in examining the concept of play, should quickly see in what marked contrast his arts lie from play. Budo training may be enjoyable. But no one who has faced the outer dangers and inner fears, the endless, irritating minor injuries and the occasional frightening big ones; no one who's gone through that and kept coming back for more could ever think of it as mere "fun." As for play's opportunity to remove us from daily life, the budo totally reject this notion. Instead, the dojo is a concentrated version of life. It offers not a means for escape from daily life, but a strenuous, unblinking confrontation with it. Nor are the budo temporary activities, indulged in on occasion, the way we would go play a round of golf, weather and time permitting, on Saturday morning. The budo like karate are an integral part of life. They demand, as well you know, almost daily practice. Their principles, we who follow them must expect, are to be polished and lived 24 hours a day. In a very real sense, practice continues for every moment of the budoka's life, whether he's in the dojo, digging in his garden, or driving down the highway.

Finally, while play has little emphasis on the discovery of deep philosophical truths, these discoveries form the very core of the process of following a martial Way. Although their physical skills were awesome, it is significant that virtually all the great budo masters of the past have been individuals with strong inclinations toward introspection and the development of a personal philosophy. (That's not to say they were wimps. On the contrary, I think they were tough and, when the situation demanded it, cold-blooded, in ways that today's competitors could never equal.) Nearly all of them made the point in books they wrote or in lectures they gave, that to engage in the techniques of karate or judo or whatever budo while mindless of their spiritual and ethical implications was not to participate in the budo at all, but rather to indulge in a perverted imitation of it.

So, if we understand now the unsuitability of "play" as a verb to describe participation in the budo, what the heck are we supposed to call it? To "follow" karate sounds more than a bit pretentious, doesn't it? If we say we "engage" in karate, it sounds just kind of awkward. I don't have a good solution. There aren't any verbs in English which correspond exactly with those used to describe training in Japanese: *renshu* or *keiko*. For lack of a better way to put it, I often find myself saying simply that "I *do* judo." Or "I'm a karate practitioner." Those still don't describe exactly what it is we do in the budo or the way in which we approach it. But it reminds me, if nothing else, that whatever we call it, the budo are a very long way from playing.

16

Move from the Hips!

Koshi ga takai-mono—"Things with high hips." When I was a young budoka, that was an insult that could tighten one's teeth in irritation. Or raise a flush of embarrassment. It meant that one was moving, executing a technique, maybe even just sitting or standing with his body balanced, top-heavy; without a low center. It was an indication too, of just how important a role the *koshi*, the hips, play in the martial arts.

There are no differences to speak of in the anatomies and physiologies of the Japanese and American (not that have any influence in the dojo, anyway). But there has evolved culturally a significant distinction in the way these two societies perceive the body, particularly in the ways those bodies generate power. In the West, we often consider a measure of strength to be the power coming from the appendicular skeleton—the shoulder girdle. That's where Atlas bore the weight of the world. It's the part of a man's body we admire when it's broad, the part we "put to the wheel" when there's work to be done. We throw a baseball from the shoulder and swing a bat from the same place. Carl Sandburg called Chicago the "city with the big shoulders" and we knew exactly what he meant.

In Japan, however, the seat of power has always been lower, in the hips. *Koshi nukeru* is an expression in Japanese for losing one's nerve. It means literally, "the hips are loose." A *koshinuke* is a person "without hips"—a coward. When cutting with a Japanese-style saw, walking across the Noh stage, or even making tea, the hips are always centered, always the source of the movement. Exercise physiologists may correct me on this. If so, I am speaking only partially from the physical perspective. Body image and mechanics have a cultural aspect as well. The truth is, if you want to see the personification of the Western concept of strength, look at the wide shoulders of most of our athletes. If you want to see the Japanese idea—and ideal—of great strength, look at the thick, muscular hips of the *sumo-*

tori. In a more abstract sense, consider Western body strength as expressed symbolically by an inverted triangle. Broad shoulders; slim hips. In contrast, turn the triangle over, into a pyramid shape, and you will have an example of strength, Japanese-style.

There are at least two precepts to be kept in mind when training, concerning the koshi, or hip region. Before I mention them, let's be sure we know what we're talking about. In the karate dojo where they let me train, I often encourage juniors to "move from your hips" and demonstrate for them what I mean. After class one evening, I was approached by a contingent of female karateka, and I learned from them that not only is my concept of the word "hips" a Japanese-influenced one, it is also from the male perspective. Women, they explained, tend to think of the hips as specifically the area right around the widest part of the buttocks. Men, I think, tend to consider the hips to include all the buttocks and the waist as well. For our purposes, though, we must use the Japanese word koshi, meaning a wider area still, one that includes every part of the trunk from the bottom of the butt well up into what we would think of as the abdomen.

The first precept is this: all movement must originate with the hips. The hips, in other words, must precede all action. The swordsman, the karateka, the judoka; all work to keep their entire body supple and relaxed. Only the hips should be kept firm and tight. That takes the "slack" out of the stance and permits instant movement without any sort of wasted "windup." And when they do move, whether it is to make an overhead slash with the sword, or a reverse punch, or a throw, they will all begin the movement from the hips, almost exactly the same way. When the hips move first, they unify the body. The koshi includes the largest muscles we have. Engaging them first allows the movement to have all the other muscles working in harmony. When the swordsman cuts, it is not just with his arms but—through his hips—the power of his whole body. The same is true for other budoka. It is not the karateka's shoulder and fist that deliver the power of his punch; it is the engagement and snapping rotation of the hips.

The second axiom involved in using the koshi is this: power must be delivered through the hips *directly* to the target. Watch a novice karateka make oi-zuki, a step-in punch. He begins in a low front stance, steps forward and punches. Inevitably, as he moves his hips will come up. That's power going away from the target. Then watch the expert make the same punch. From his beginning stance all the way through the step forward into the punch, his koshi will be exactly the same height from the floor. He squeezes his thighs and allows his hips to move in a straight, horizontal line. No power is lost or misdirected. The same results tend to occur when the two, expert and beginner, kick. The beginner kicks with his leg only. Often, in fact, his hips are sticking out to the rear even as he tries to kick to the front. The black belt, though, will stretch, putting his hips behind the kick. He has more reach and he is capable of delivering more effectively his power.

Traditional Japanese life provided numerous opportunities to strengthen and develop the koshi. In a recent issue of *Kenchiku Zasshi* (*Architect Magazine*), a writer observed that the Japanese in the old days spent 80 percent of his time indoors on the floor. He worked while squatting and ate while kneeling. And of course, he slept on the floor, too. Not only did all this sort of activity constantly strengthen his hips; it contributed to the cultural image of being like that pyramid. The Japanese of old spent a lot of time low to the ground, and it is not surprising that his combative arts would be oriented around the lower parts of his body.

To the well-trained budoka, the average Westerner looks dreadfully unbalanced and top-heavy. A high center of balance, to that same budoka, is often a sign of emotional and spiritual instability as well. That's why the phrase *koshi ga takai-mono* is such a penetrating criticism. Its connotations go far deeper than the physical. To move from the hips is to act from a position of equilibrium. And to originate one's behavior from that kind of poise, whether in the dojo, or in life itself, is the essence of the Way.

17

Karate, the Martial Art That's Not (Part 1)

I was having lunch with an editor of a magazine devoted to karate. He was buying, not something editors are given to do for writers, and we were at a little, family-run Thai restaurant in Los Angeles, back in the days when you could only get really good, really hot Thai food, the way it is supposed to be made, in places like that. It was delicious. So I was making an effort not to be too obnoxious. Still, I could not resist, looking through the latest edition we had at the table with us, pointing out a certain inaccuracy. The publication was, according to its masthead, a journal of the "State of the Martial Art." My editor was curious when I observed that of course Japanese karate was neither.

"Neither what?" he asked.

"Neither martial, nor an art," I replied.

"What?" His eyebrows furrowed. It is easier to get an editor to buy lunch than it is to puzzle one. I was delighted with myself. How, he wanted to know, could I think such a thing? Well, I did. And I do. And here's why.

It is, superficially, a matter of semantics. Which is not to say it is not important. Those who dismiss disagreements with the scoff that "it's just semantics," are often unwilling to see that semantics are vital if we are to understand meaning. This is especially vital when we are dealing in terms, as with the Japanese we use in the dojo, that we have translated into English. We must be very careful to remember that translated words are approximations. Otherwise, we can lose sight of what it is we are after. . . .

The best translation of "martial" into Japanese is *bu*. As a prefix, bu occurs in many words with which the average martial artist is familiar in addition to, of course, budo, or "martial Ways." We see it in *bushido*, the "Way of the *bushi*," the Japanese warrior's code of ethics. A *buke* is a hereditary military family. As for the indigenous martial skills of Japan, they are roughly divided into the bujutsu, the classical fighting schools of the feudal samurai and the budo, which have a more modern and more explicitly spiritual energy. Significantly, however, the prefix of bu in Japanese refers only to native Japanese martial techniques. Chinese or European martial arts, for instance, are not described in Japanese as *bu*-forms. Neither, to be technical, would be an Okinawan method of combat, of which karate unquestionably is. (Both Japanese and Okinawan historians generally agree on this: some Okinawans in fact, are irritated when their native weaponry arts are called *kobudo*, a Japanese word meaning, approximately, "old martial Ways." That word indicates older *Japanese* weaponry forms, they insist, and they prefer theirs to be called by the correct phrase in Okinawan: *te-gua*.)

I explained this to my editor. He argued, as I thought he would, that while karate was originally Okinawan, it has been altered and adapted since its introduction to Japan in the early 20th century, and it now conforms to the philosophies and methods of the Japanese budo. That argument has its flaws, however, at least two of them. Remember that bu refers not specifically to "combat" or "fighting" but to that which is related to the military or martial caste of old Japan. Okinawan karate was never an art of the warrior class. It was a method of fighting practiced by Ryukyuans, most of them farmers or fishermen. It is, in origin and intent, a *civilian* method of self-defense. (There was, to be absolutely historically accurate, an elite caste in the hierarchy of Okinawan civilization. They referred to themselves, in some instances, as bushi, in imitation of the warrior class in Japan. There was also, during the feudal era in Okinawa, a military class of sorts, devoted primarily to maintaining the order and power of the emperors of the island chain. Karate, though, has scant connection to either of these two groups.)

To affix the connotation of "civil" rather than "military" (or "martial") to an art like karate is not a comment on the effectiveness or value of karate. Most of the combative arts of mainland China, *kung fu, tai chi chuan*, and the like, are, as well, civilian in their origins. Recognizing that karate is an art used by non-military people does not discredit it at all. It merely places karate in its proper perspective as a fighting art. Unlike judo (which descended clearly from *jujutsu*), kendo *(kenjutsu)*, and *kyudo (kyujutsu)*, karate cannot claim a classical Japanese heritage. It cannot, technically speaking, be counted as a "martial" discipline, then, at least not in the Japanese sense of that word.

Whether karate is or isn't an *art* is a question more problematic. Yet once again, if we adhere to the definition of that concept in Japanese we once again must conclude that the answer is negative. The Japanese word *jutsu* is usually translated as "art," and whether that's accurate—the word *gei* is probably closer to the idea of art we have when we use that word in English, while jutsu refers more precisely to "techniques" or "skills"—it is contrasted with the idea of *Do*, or the Way, in an important way. Jutsu, as I said, indicates a craft, or skill, or discipline. It does not carry the philosophical implication of self-perfection that is the essence of the Do. Had there been a "karate-jutsu" then, it would have involved only the attainment of fighting skills, devoid of the spiritual goals that galvanize the budo.

Was there karate-jutsu? Up until well into the 20th century, most Okinawans referred to their primary fighting art simply as *te* ("hand") or *tode* ("China hand"): probably it was called karate-jutsu by the more educated among karate practitioners when they tried to explain karate to the Japanese. But Gichin Funakoshi and his contemporaries who introduced the art to Japan sought not to emphasize karate's physical skills while ignoring its spiritual values. So they consciously avoided affixing the jutsu suffix to karate. They presented it as an evolving form of other, better-known martial Ways, stressing moral and philosophical aspects that removed it from anything resembling a feudal-era bujutsu. So while there might conceivably have been an Okinawan form of karate-jutsu and might still be, the Japanese version is karate-*do*; not an art, but a Way.

I prefaced this by admitting that we were engaged in a discussion of semantics. For the sake of convenience, we all include karate-do with the other martially inspired budo, and we call it a martial "art," for the same reason. That's okay, so long as we know there *is* a distinction. If the karateka is to understand where his karate-do is today, though, he must be quite sure of where and what it was originally, and what its forefathers ancient and modern intended it to be. Names are convenient, but they should not confuse us. So, while we'll agree to continue to use "martial art" to describe karate, we should also bear in mind it is neither. Which leads us to ask, what the heck then is it?

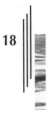

Karate, the Martial Art That's Not (Part 2)

It may sound odd that the best-known of the martial arts, karate-do, is neither martial nor an art. As I have suggested, though, karate was developed as a *civilian* rather than a military or "martial" form of combat. I argued too, that karate presents itself as a budo, a Way, instead of a *bujutsu*, or art. And that left us wondering, just what *is* karate?

By way of answer, I would like you first to consider a word which is rarely heard outside certain circles in Japan but one which has deep meaning there. That word is *mingei*. In Japanese, mingei is a term referring to the "people's arts" or "folk arts." It was brought into usage in Japan by Soetsu Yanagi, an artist and connoisseur of post-war Japan. When Japan lost the war it was threatened as well with the loss of much of the artistic and aesthetic spirit that had motivated artists and craftsmen in that country for centuries. The Japanese, having been so thoroughly disillusioned with the lies of the government about Japanese superiority in all things, rushed to embrace everything that was Western, just as they had earlier, when the first contact with the United States in the 1800s ended more than three centuries of isolation. Post-war Japan got a constitution, women's rights, and modern, safe factories. Unfortunately, in the bargain the Japanese also got a taste of all that was trendy, mass-produced, and superficial.

In the midst of Japan's modernization, some fought the tide. Soetsu Yanagi led a movement that sought to retain the old and traditional in Japanese art and culture. He found a special value in the simple, utilitarian crafts of the country folk. In fact, largely through his efforts museums devoted to folk art were built, native craftsmen were recognized, and a unique facet of Japanese culture was preserved. This was mingei, the crafts of the common folk.

Although they are not usually so identified, such skills as regional folk dancing and music are really mingei, too. And so, I think, is karate. No doubt it is odd at first blush to be throwing a violent form of combat into the same cultural basket as country-style pottery, or weaving, or wood carving. But karate is rightfully considered folk art: it meets well every criteria.

Karate is unquestionably a product of country people. Unlike the professional warrior arts of feudal Japan, like swordsmanship (kenjutsu) and grappling in armor (jujutsu), karate has no aristocratic origins. It is a craft of farmers and fishermen who were close to the land and sea and who chose by no coincidence, to name their kata after such natural elements as might be found there.

Karate, like the mingei of pottery or weaving, is also utilitarian. The potter and weaver did not create objects merely to be admired or to decorate. They served a useful function. For the same reason exactly, pretentious costumes and combatively pointless acrobatics had no place in the peasant's karate. He would have tended to regard them as vulgar and more importantly, as dangerous. He had no wish to draw attention to himself, and his techniques were purely and expertly functional. Mingei, however, did seek beauty as a natural by-product of utility. Sometimes it was only the simple abstract designs of mountains or rivers found in Okinawan *bingata* dyeing; others had great intricacy, like the dragons molded into ordinary roofing tiles. Karate too, included graceful, aesthetically pleasing movements. Its beauty transcends function, as is always true of the mingei.

While they are outwardly simplistic, rough, earthenware bowls or hand-crafted wooden tools, by their very nature mingei reject superficiality. The closer one examines, say, Okinawan dance, for instance, the more reflections of the culture behind the dance are revealed. To watch the undulations of *kumi-odori* (an Okinawan folk dance) is to see, in artistic form, the harvesting and planting motions of ancient times on Okinawa. To train and to be taught truly the meaning behind karate's kata is to gain insight into the kind of combat engaged in by the Ryukyuans, to understand how they passed their fighting knowledge down and how they integrated it into their lives.

Karate has come to be perceived in many ways since leaving its homeland, some of them good and worthwhile, others a waste of time and worse. Yet no matter how we view karate or what we call it, it is interesting to look at this art under an unusual light now and then. That is my purpose in presenting karate here as a folk craft. I think karate *is* a mingei; that is actually its cultural niche. And those of us who practice it that way may eventually come to understand just what special craftsmen were those karateka who preceded us, and what a special craft it was they left for us.

19

A Working Definition of *Ki*

Nishimoto osho was the Buddhist priest who was responsible for tending to the spiritual needs of a rather large congregation back in the sixties. He oversaw funerals, some weddings, and various other Buddhist celebrations for believers all over the Midwest. He was also a judo *godan*, a fifth-degree black belt who served as a referee at a lot of the judo tournaments we used to have. As an osho, or priest, he also saw himself as an unofficial Youth Counselor of sorts, to us boys in judo, knocking our heads together—sometimes literally—when we got out of line. Even those of us who weren't Buddhist were more than a little intimidated by Nishimoto. He never talked a lot. His idea of leading us boys in the right direction was to provide an example—and to be quick and decisive when he thought we were headed in the wrong direction.

Nishimoto had a look, a glare that could freeze you. Back in the sixties, as young teenagers, some of us had a tendency to be *kuchi ga sugiru:* "smart-mouthed" is the best translation. I cannot remember how many times a remark I deemed snappy and urbane was already forming on my lips when a hard glance from Nishimoto made me swallow it.

He wasn't the complete stereotype of the boot camp drill instructor, though. Nishimoto osho also had an odd sense of humor, and if there was a chance for a practical joke, he wasn't the guy to let it pass. One afternoon, in the dressing room of a university where we'd just finished a judo tournament, we were all changing and the osho, sitting on a bench in his underwear, suddenly announced that he was really polishing his *ki*. Are there readers who do not know the word? Ki, or *chi,* in Chinese, is that mysterious, ineffable "power" that transcends physical force. It is the "chi" of *chi-kung* (or the *qi* of *qi gong* if the murky swamp waters of Pinyin float your boat); the "ki" of *aikido*. Some devote their lives to mastering it. Others insist it's a complete fraud. Nishimoto osho, though, had announced that his was in fine shape, and whatever our personal understanding or opinions were surrounding ki, we knew enough to keep them to ourselves in his presence.

"Put your fists on top of one another, your arms extended out in front," Nishimoto told one of the guys, then told him to tighten his muscles, to try to keep the fists where they were. I will separate them, the osho said, using my ki extended through the tips of my forefingers. Sure enough, he put one finger on the boy's top fist, the other, on the other side, on the bottom, and rapped both fists. They scissored apart instantly.

Try it. No matter how strong you are, even a child can knock your fists apart. But then, Nishimoto told us that he'd perfected his ki and was able to prevent anyone from separating his fists. Sure enough, he held them out and we tried it. First with just our fingers, then using our whole open hands to try to whack his fists apart. His fists rocked from side to side with the force of our strikes, but they stayed absolutely together. He let us try this for several minutes, until we were all awed by the power of his ki. Then he showed us its mysterious secret: when putting his fists together, he extended the bottom thumb and held it in the fist of his top.

He must have laughed for twenty minutes.

I suspect many readers believe the above anecdote pretty much sums up the whole mystical world of ki. Hard to blame them for their cynicism. Ki is kind of the "Oriental" version of ESP, telekinesis, or half a dozen other "paranormal" skills that have been foisted off—I mean, presented—to the public in the past several decades. Dressed up in the esoterica of the Far East, ki-power has had an enormous attraction for many of us. It has been tough on the true believers, however. First of all, it didn't take long for professional magicians to catch on to the tricks of remarkable ki-power. It's now common to see them performing what were once described as mystical feats of ki, attainable only through long years of mental and physical training.

That "Shaolin monk" up on the stage bending a solid steel spear into a big U while its sharp tip was pressed against his throat was pretty impressive, but it lost a little of the shine when you saw a balding, potbellied Mr. Misterio do the same *shtick* at the Las Vegas "World o' Magic" in some seedy casino on the Strip. The "unbendable arm" routine wore thin the first time you realized it was a simple matter of leverage. (If you don't think so, instead of standing with your arm extended over the tester's shoulder, next time sit in seiza, on the floor. Have him stand to the side, one hand palm down on your elbow, the other palm up on your wrist, and let him crank. Amazing how fast that unbendable arm becomes more flexible than a Hollywood movie exec's morals.)

I have my own ideas about ki. If nothing else, I have a lot of experience in being hit; I've been hit hard, by guys using purely physical, muscular force. And I've been hit by guys completely relaxed, who were using something else. And I can tell you there is a difference. I can tell you that, but I won't. There's no sense arguing about it, and if you don't accept ki, there's room enough in the world for both of us. What I would like to offer is a definition of ki that might at least allow believers and skeptics to talk about it without getting into fistfights.

Let's think of it this way: ki is the most efficient way of moving, performing some action, using the least number of muscles, tendons, or ligaments needed. Using the least to get the most. Using nothing that isn't absolutely necessary for the task. And using what is necessary to its absolute maximum. Consider this analogy: Back when telephones became common, it required an operator to plug in a connection. It was slow, cumbersome; relatively inefficient. Things got smoother and faster as technology improved. The digital age arrived. Now we can call the other side of the planet in less time than it takes to call the kids in for supper. Equipment has gotten smaller, infinitely more efficient. When you began learning technique in the dojo, you were like one of those old-fashioned phones. You used a lot of power, with relatively inefficient results. As you got better and better, what happened? You wasted less energy, became more efficient. That process continues as you progress. The master is like a cable modem (or whatever new technology comes out between the time I write this and the time you read it); he uses absolutely the least muscle in the most efficient way. In a sense, at least, he might be thought of as using his ki.

I realize this definition does not take into account the supposedly miraculous, paranormal qualities of ki, healing with a touch, throwing people without touching them, and so on. My hope, though, is that it will provide you with another way of looking at the whole concept of ki and of implementing at least some aspects of it—or of what it's supposed to be—into your own training.

20

How Much Would You Pay for All the Secrets of the Martial Arts?

Wait, don't answer yet: if you act now we'll also throw in this handy combination cheese grater/hair dryer. . . . Call now, operators are standing by.

This approach appears to be a popular method of advertising the martial arts, particularly when trying to solicit people to come to special instructional clinics. It is common to see advertisements which promise to instruct in the "real" techniques hidden in kata, or the "actual combat applications" of this martial Way or that. Now look, fellow consumers; it is no business of mine how you part with you cash. (One of my own ancestors is still celebrated in our family for choosing to invest not in a fledgling company called AT&T, but instead sinking his money into a scheme to crossbreed cantaloupes with pineapples, so I am obviously not a source of investment counseling.) But do you really believe the "secrets" of something as ancient and complex as the martial arts can or will be distributed like merchandise at a bargain basement sale?

I do not mean to imply that qualified teachers at clinics mightn't be able to instruct students in a number of areas to improve their skills in a variety of ways. Just last night I said goodbye to some of the JKA karateka who let me train with them. They will spend a week in Chicago at a clinic given by the JKA teacher Hidetaka Nishiyama, and they will return with improved training ideas and a lot of other points for us all to practice. These kinds of clinics are usually conducted by and for specific arts or styles. They are usually geared with the prior experience of the participants in mind. (Not so the one I read about a while back, proposing to teach a number of "classical sword kata" to students who may well have not even known how to grip a sword for all the teacher leading the clinic knew. Come to think of it, that limitation probably applied as well to the "grandmaster" at that questionable event.) In addition, well run clinics by established and credible teachers provide a chance to see outstanding instructors and to meet with fellow practitioners. They are imminently worthwhile. I am referring instead to those seminars claiming to reveal the hithertofore concealed methods of an art to anyone with the entry fee and energy to walk through the door. Martial artists expecting those revelations need to understand what the *kuden*, the orally transmitted "secrets" of the martial arts are, and how they are traditionally passed on.

One distinguishing characteristic of the Japanese martial Ways is that they absolutely must be conveyed in a "hands on" way. Scrolls, written instructions, even the videotapes that have become extremely popular as a teaching source: all are purely supplemental. The budo are taught, at the higher levels at least, the same way all arts have been taught in Japan for centuries. Only by "sharing shadows" with one's master, by training that closely with him for a long time, can the student begin to acquire his own skills. All the time this training process is unfolding, the master is evaluating his student's progress. This is an enormously complicated task. It must be balanced just right. The teacher must never give more than can be digested by the student, never leave him starving for new challenges.

When he judges the time to be right, the teacher will begin to drop morsels of information in an understated, apparently offhand way. The aikidoka is told that "by the way," his *kote gaeshi* (wrist reversal) will be more effective "if you turn your elbows like this. . . ." The kendoka is taken aside quietly during practice one day and told "strike your opponent's wrist at this angle and you'll numb it; he can't hold his *shinai*." In a private moment, the karate sensei shows his disciple "twist your block when it contacts his wrist here and it'll cause his eyes to water for a second, opening him for a counter."

At first, the student will view these tips as odd, unconnected scraps of information. Gradually, more and more of them will be dropped on him. The longer he trains, the more will be revealed. They are not specific lessons. Nor are they given to every student at the same time. In fact, some students will never receive them at all. If they fail to show interest, if they lack the patience or attitudes the sensei deems necessary, they may be left out. The budo are not democratic. Not everyone in the dojo gets exactly the same instruction. But this kind of highly individualized teaching has a specific purpose. The kuden, the oral teachings, give the sincere, hardworking student an edge over those who don't try as hard. They reward him for his efforts. Most importantly, the kuden make the student conscious of the vast body of knowledge that has been accumulated within the traditional martial Ways. If he gobbles the kuden smugly and rests on this new knowledge, he'll likely get no more. If he absorbs them humbly and continues rigorous training, more will come his way. He will eventually realize that they have been passed down to his teacher exactly the way his master imparts them to him. Like all the traditional arts, excellence is attained drop by drop in the budo.

When I began training with my sensei, part of my duties were in helping with the cooking around the house. Over the years I helped several men and women cook all sorts of Japanese food and I learned to watch them carefully and to copy their recipes when I liked what they prepared. I noticed that every good Japanese cook had his or her own recipe for *tsuke-jiru*. Tsuke-jiru is a broth in which noodles and all sorts of other foods are cooked. It is, in some ways, like the broth of a soup. Making a good tsuke-jiru is the sign of a good cook. It is a skill that takes a long time to develop and to personalize. No matter how you do it, you must take care. Try to slop a tsuke-jiru together quickly and you'll have a mess with half a dozen flavors all fighting one another. A truly superior tsuke-jiru must be simmered slowly, all day long. As it cooks, bits of seaweed and dried fish are added, not all at once; only when the broth is ready for the next ingredient. The result is smoothly blended and delicious.

I don't know what real skills might be imparted at the kind of clinics where all sorts of alleged secrets and hidden techniques are dumped upon customers on one or two afternoons. I have not attended any. So I can't say. But I do wonder what kind of cooks the teachers of these clinics must be, and I wonder too, about the value of their hastily brewed and hurriedly served products.

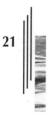

21

Now and Zen (Part 1)

Underarm deodorant does not cause cancer.

Shaven street rats are not sold to tourists in Mexico as Chihuahuas.

You can't get "high" on aspirin and Coke.

Okay, now that these perennially popular myths have been duly addressed, let me nominate a couple more.

1. The samurai were never, in any large numbers at all, enthusiastic practitioners of Zen.

2. The connection between Zen and the Japanese budo is not ancient; it is, in fact, not too much older than the Hula-Hoop.

Some background: Zen is a form of Buddhism. In a very, very simple context, Buddhism teaches that mankind's suffering comes not from an original disobedience to God as those of us who are Christians believe, but rather from illusion. We suffer, the Buddha taught, because of illusionary desires. I'd be happy if I was rich. I'd be happy if my view of my toes was unimpeded by my belly. I'd be happy if I'd married Cindy Crawford. Or at least spent some real quality time with her. These are illusions we construct around ourselves, which prevent us from perceiving reality. Seeing through to reality is a way of eliminating suffering, the Buddha taught. To that end, Buddhism uses several approaches. Some involve chanting of sacred scriptures; others focus on personal actions. Some, most noticeably Zen, employ meditation. By focusing our minds on illogical questions, called koan, or on meditative exercises designed to rid the practitioner of extraneous thoughts, the Zen Buddhist strives to concentrate consciousness on the present, on seeing reality free of illusions, living each moment fully for itself.

Zen was introduced to Japan in the 12th century, from China. Earlier forms of Buddhism had appealed to the aristocracy, others to the commoners in Japan.

Zen was largely a monastic approach to Buddhism. It was centered in Kyoto and Kamakura, where the shogun was then located. Because of his patronage, Zen very quickly prospered and several temples devoted to it were built. Since the Zen priesthood was better educated than the laity and certainly better than the average samurai of that period, they served as advisors to the shogun and to the leaders of the warrior class. Some historians have mistakenly concluded that the samurai were attracted to Zen for this reason and because when some samurai retired, they entered the priesthood themselves. Historians have also incorrectly surmised that because Zen stresses self-discipline and an austere lifestyle, qualities admired by the samurai as well, that the samurai were devoted to this sect of Buddhism. This is demonstrably wrong and you can see why if you'll think about circumstances during the feudal period in Japan.

The rise of the warrior class was marked by warfare. From the 10th century until the start of the 17th, Japan saw a lot of war. Samurai lived with the knowledge that they might be dead the next military campaign, or from an unexpected attack in the next hour. They simply did not have the luxury of spending several years sitting in meditation to develop a spirit to deal with that. That's what Zen practice demanded. It was a long, tedious, trying process, tackling illusion through the medium of meditation. Zen was not a practical approach for a guy who needed to see through those illusions right now. The samurai may have respected Zen Buddhism. He surely relied on the priesthood of that sect during some periods of Japanese history, for education or advice. But in their letters, personal documents, in their *densho* (transmission scrolls of martial arts schools), there are very, very few references at all to Zen by the samurai class. This leaves us with two questions. In what spiritual or religious training *did* the samurai engage? And, how did the notion that the arts of the samurai and Zen are inextricably intertwined become so common? The first question we'll leave for the next chapter. One answer to the second is that Yagyu Munenori (1571–1646), the second headmaster of the Yagyu Shinkage ryu, a school of swordsmanship and martial strategy, was a friend and disciple of the Zen Buddhist priest Takuan Soho (1573–1645). Takuan wrote some treatises and letters to his student, using the analogy of swordsmanship and martial strategy to explain Zen. (Did the legendary swordsman Miyamoto Musashi also learn from Takuan? Yes. In a fictional serialized novel later made into a movie. In real life the two almost certainly never even met.)

Because the Yagyu Shinkage ryu enjoyed the patronage of the shogun, it was enormously influential. The commentaries Takuan wrote to Munenori (he also wrote similar letters to other swordsmen and *daimyo*) were widely read. Conversely, the densho, the curriculum scrolls of most ryu, were kept secret from nonmembers. So the general public, exposed to Takuan's writings, assumed a close Zen/budo connection. Martial artists reinforced this in the post-feudal period, especially kendoka, who employed Zen terminology because it clarified their philosophies about their arts and because using such spiritual terms elevated the status of those arts.

When budo was introduced to the West in a big way after World War II, the supposed relationship between Zen and the martial arts was further solidified in popular imagination. The scholar Daisetsu Suzuki (he was neither a Zen practitioner nor a martial artist) wrote his enormously successful *Zen and Japanese Culture*, devoting two long chapters to Zen and swordsmanship. Eugene Herrigel, a German who was not proficient in Japanese, briefly studied kyudo in Japan during the 1930s and published an equally successful book, *Zen and the Art of Archery*. Both books used the medium of Zen to explain budo. Virtually all that has been written since in English can be traced back to translations of Takuan's writings or these two books.

If the modern budoka wishes to brew his cup of budo with a Zen flavor or to teach it so, that is his choice, of course. But if he does so assuming a long historical and spiritual connection with the samurai of old, he is mistaken and does a disservice to the warrior spirit of Japan.

22

Now and Zen (Part 2)

In the previous chapter, we examined the popular notion that the martial arts of Japan and Zen are as inseparable as the Captain and Tenille, matzos and chicken soup, manila and envelopes. The notion has sprung, we noted, from books linking Zen to the cultural milieu of the feudal samurai. If these books are to be believed, the samurai sat in *zazen* several hours a day, contemplating nothingness or the sound of one hand clapping or *something* in their search for enlightenment and pausing only long enough to perform feats of derring-do out on the battlefield or in duels. Today's budoka, it has become firmly established in the minds of many, many practitioners all over the world, are the spiritual descendants of these Zen samurai.

Zen parables are frequently recited in martial arts dojo, and they fill page after page of books written about budo. Many schools include some kind of meditation in their training and students are exhorted to take attitudes reflective of Zen philosophy, even when it isn't exactly clear just what those should be. We noted that such a connection does not exist historically, however. The samurai were not particularly enamored with Zen. There is little evidence they engaged in much formal Zen training.

So what spirituality, we ended the last chapter by asking, *did* inform the samurai? The answer, in large measure, is *mikkyo*. Some readers may know of it. But it has never been as popular in the West as other forms of Buddhism. So let's back up a bit. To begin: Zen is an exoteric form of Buddhism. So are most other forms of Buddhism. Jodo, Shinshu; these are all various forms of exoteric Japanese Buddhism. None of them involves any sort of esoterica in the sense that arcane, secret teachings are imparted to the disciple as part of his religious instruction. They are also exoteric in that their teachings are transmitted to anyone seeking them. One exception in Japanese Buddhism is mikkyo, also called Shingon. It is perhaps the only true form of esoteric Buddhism with deep roots in that country.

As we discussed previously, Buddhism teaches basically that suffering comes through illusions. A good martial arts-related example would be the fellow who suddenly appears on the street in front of you with a knife. Your imagination goes into overdrive. You wonder what plans he has. You worry about the wicked-looking knife, about the pain it could cause. You fret about not having trained hard enough to meet this circumstance. All these thoughts are illusion. The truth is simply that there is a man in front of you with a knife. You must deal with the reality, not with the product of your imagination. In one way or another, all forms of Buddhism confront our tendencies towards illusions.

Mikkyo's approach is through various psychological and neurological exercises, many of them featuring the invocation of supernatural powers. There is a whole pantheon of Buddhist deities who may be summoned, according to mikkyo teachings, who will impart power or protection. These are called upon through different mediums. The mikkyo adept may focus on votive art—mandala—or through chants or by physical acts or motions. The best known of these are the *kuji-kiri,* the "finger weaving" some of you may have seen in books. Each deity is represented by a particular way of weaving one's fingers together. In a crude sense, these can be thought of as "spells." On a more sophisticated level, they are complex rituals designed to instill confidence, presence of mind, and a spirit of equanimity in the face of a threat or danger. The practitioner of mikkyo uses representative art, chants or special words, or the kuji-kiri to call upon specific deities that will impart strength or an ability to read an opponent's mind or as a form of protection.

Mikkyo's influences on the martial arts are not easy to see, especially in our modern era. There are castles in Japan that have, hidden away somewhere on the foundation stones or other places, mikkyo inscriptions. Armor and weapons of that period are sometimes decorated with mikkyo symbology. Scrolls detailing the lineages or techniques of a classical martial arts tradition are often decorated with depictions of mikkyo deities. In initiation ceremonies and at the presentation of licenses in the remaining schools of feudal era combative arts, mikkyo paraphernalia is often present. It is, in fact, a rich tradition. But it's one that's hidden from ordinary view.

Mikkyo, though it has a following in the country, is still the most uncommon form of Buddhism in Japan. Devotees pass through a long period of initiation. In feudal Japan, many if not most classical martial arts contained in their curricula mikkyo teachings of one form or another. These "secrets" were not revealed to outsiders. Adherents believed the rituals imparted power and they were loath to share that.

It's easy to see why the samurai would have so enthusiastically embraced mikkyo. It offered comfort and protection and a sense of well-being that was, more or less, immediately available. (Unlike the rewards of Zen which were attained after years of effort.) It was an elite form of spirituality, which naturally appealed to a class like the samurai who saw themselves as a caste quite different from others in Japan. It required initiation into its secrets, very much like the martial arts they practiced.

With the end of feudalism and the concurrent rise of popular forms of combative arts like the modern budo, mikkyo did not translate well. It was certainly disdained by many modern budoka of late 19th-century Japan like judo's Jigoro Kano who, with limited experience in classical schools, would have had little exposure to it anyway. The spiritual aspects of their budo were directed more in the direction of a social ethic, infused by Confucian thought. Later, as we discussed previously, Zen became incorporated into the budo, grafted on for various reasons. The role of Zen was further magnified by Westerners who employed it as a part of their training. Consequently, Zen and the budo are thought to be intimately linked and many well-meaning writers have written volumes explaining the "connection." You know better.

23

The Dojo—Visitors Not Welcome

An acquaintance is in the process of renovating an old carriage house into what promises to be a very nice traditional dojo. The structure itself is perfect for a martial arts training hall. It is over a century old, located on the precincts of some property that was a big farm at one time. The land right around the carriage house is already being cultivated into a beautiful garden inspired by the *shakkei* style of formal gardens found in many temples in Japan. There is a stream running through the garden, emptying into a little pond that has already been stocked with large, lazily swimming *koi* the colors of bright brocades. Inside, a planked floor of oak has been put down, with plenty of give in it so it will not be too hard on the bare feet and legs and spines of the people who will be training on it. There has been space set aside at the front of the dojo for a *tokonoma*, an alcove that will hold flower arrangements and a calligraphic scroll. On one wall is a weapons rack that will be filled with wooden swords and staffs and so on. And of course, there is a shelf being installed at the front that will hold the *kamiza*, the Shinto shrine that will house the spirits of the area and of the arts that will be practiced before it. The dojo, in short, has everything needed for a proper training hall for the martial Ways.

We were doing some work on the new dojo the other day when a friend of the builder's dropped by, one who does not practice the budo. He looked around, admired the floor, and then, "Nice place," he noted, "but," he asked, "where will the visitors sit?" There was not, he commented, any place for observers in the dojo. No visitor gallery; no place set aside for chairs or for standing around and watching the action out on the floor.

None of us working on the dojo had an immediate answer for him. We all *knew* the answer, mind you. But there wasn't any really polite way to tell him. The answer is—and this will probably surprise most martial artists who train in a typical commercial dojo of the sort found in most cities in the United States—that a properly built dojo does not need and should not have a place for visitors.

As I said, this is something that will strike many people studying the martial arts in this country as very odd. Indeed, if you go into the average commercial martial arts school you will find that nearly all of them have a section where there are seats for those who come to watch. Check the advertising for martial arts schools in the phone book and you will find this invitation "Visitors Welcome!" almost as frequently as you will see the guarantee of "No Contracts!" In fact, newcomers to the martial arts are often advised to "shop around." They are routinely encouraged to visit different schools and to be suspicious of those that do not welcome them cheerily.

So is something shady going on at my friend's dojo? No, nor is anything amiss at the majority of strictly traditional dojo in Japan and elsewhere which provide no special place for visitors and which discourage casual observers from coming in in the first place. The reason for this attitude is that a traditional martial arts training hall is not meant as a place of business. It is not for profit, nor is it designed to "attract" students or to make them comfortable. The dojo is almost always meant for a limited number of individuals who are serious about following a martial Way and who wish to do so undisturbed. Most forms of the budo are dangerous for the practitioner and injuries can easily occur if concentration is not maintained. All forms of the budo require periods of intense focus. The fewer the distractions, the better. Most walk-in spectators are nothing more than that: distractions. And since these dojo are invariably small (and wish to remain so), there is simply no room for idle observers, in any sense of the word.

But the most important reason why there is no room for casual visitors at the traditional budo dojo is this: the budo are an activity, a discipline, for doers. They are not for watchers. There is no such thing as an armchair budoka, although you may have seen those who are trying to become one. Sitting in the visitor's section, they are the most skilled of experts—if their authoritative-sounding comments are any evidence. But somehow they just never make it out onto the training floor. The commercial dojo must tolerate these types well as all manner of gawkers and spectators, because among them may always be some potentially serious students, and those students are necessary for everything from paying the light bills to becoming the next generation of teachers.

There are other reasons why the commercial training hall must allow spectators and even encourage them. Most of these establishments depend upon large children's classes to pay the bills. Parents would be reluctant to allow their children to go regularly to some place where the parents themselves were not welcome. Then too, some of these schools may be renting space in other places, dance studios, gymnastics clubs, or public school gyms, where seating and other amenities for spectators are already installed. These situations are understandable. Still, it is important for the serious budoka to see why, in an ideal dojo, there will never be rows of chairs or non-practitioners standing around and watching.

The members of a traditional dojo do not deny that at least some visitors might be sincere, and might want to watch prior to applying to join the school. Nor should the serious budoka practicing at a real dojo ever be insensitive to those with an honest curiosity. But most of them feel that to make a special effort to cater to the needs or desires of visitors would be to divert the emphasis on the dojo away from its central and only real purpose: to follow the Way. These individuals do not look upon their dojo as a commercial enterprise. They do not need new students to pay the bills, preferring to keep their dojo sufficiently modest so they can maintain it themselves. They approach their budo with the attitude that it is a Way worthy enough that potential students will not need a spectator's view of training. Others wanting to study the budo will be found, the members of this kind of dojo believe, among those willing to wait patiently at the doorstep.

There is no sense in denying that this attitude smacks of elitism. It does. But then again, the numbers of students studying at Oxford, for instance, are not all that large. Cambridge doesn't advertise. Traditional budoka like to think of their dojo as no less special or exclusive.

The reluctance of the budo dojo to make accommodations for visitors should not be translated to mean that those truly determined have no chance to gain entrance to watch training. Even the strictest of training halls has visitors from time to time. Often these people will be friends of members or others who are known through work or other connections. Those who do visit the traditional dojo, however, are almost always individuals who understand that they are not happily received guests, but tolerated disruptions. Their presence is politely suffered, and they should understand that. The intelligent outside observer of budo training realizes he may be admitted to the dojo for an abbreviated glimpse at what goes on there. Yet unless he's willing to make the commitment to join in wholeheartedly, he knows it is a place he will never be consistently welcome.

24

R-E-S-P-E-C-T

Two incidents within the space of a month.

—An advertising firm e-mails me. I've been referred to them; they're launching a new "samurai character" to advertise some client's products, and they are planning a party with a Japanese theme to introduce the character. They would like, specifically, some kind of "samurai martial art" demonstration. They wish to know of me "what kind of services you provide and what are your fees."

—From a university comes a brochure, inviting me to a weekend symposium on Japanese art and aesthetics. A trio of renowned professors will be speaking and making presentations. A display of Meiji era pottery will be exhibited; there are other programs and talks planned. The brochure notes, in smaller print down at the bottom that, in addition, "if weather permits, there will be a demonstration of kendo" on a university lawn.

Do you see a correlation in these two incidents? If not, let me point it out each demeans the budo. Each relegates the budo to the status of entertainment, sideshow spectacle, or amusing diversion. Neither treats the budo as respectable or dignified.

I hasten to add that there is nothing malicious in these incidents. Nobody deliberately set out to demonstrate disrespect for the martial arts. Neither the PR guy nor the university department that drafted the brochure for the Japanese art program was slinging mud in our eye. In part, that's what makes these situations so difficult to deal with. We have to try to make people understand what budo is all about, but we must understand from our end that their misconceptions about it aren't all that tough to explain.

Many years ago I dealt with a woman organizing a Japanese cultural festival. Needing "martial arts," she had flipped through the phone book and found an ad she liked for a local *taekwondo* school. Now taekwondo is just a dandy art for those interested in it, and I can think of several public gatherings where a demonstration of it would be appropriate. A Japanese cultural festival ain't one of them. I made an effort to point this out to her. I observed too, that she'd invited a Shito ryu karate group the year before, one that had been received well by audiences and put on a fine demonstration. Yes, she agreed. But she wanted, she said, "to give someone else a chance."

The woman's egalitarian impulses notwithstanding, I suspect she misplaced the number of the Shito ryu dojo and didn't want to go to the trouble of finding it. It was "martial arts" and it just wasn't that important. Even when it is given center stage, as when the PR fellow wanted a demonstration to highlight his party, the actual content is not given much consideration. For him, it was the spectacle of the event, the value of budo as an entertainment.

I hope I'm not breaking news to you, but the public doesn't take martial arts very seriously. Movies and TV form their perspective, almost entirely. They may have a cousin or a nephew who "does karate." If you asked ten adults at random what personal connection they have with a martial art, I'd bet the majority will say either that they did it when they were kids or they know a child of a friend or relative who is involved. Already, in their minds, budo is something for adolescents, not a serious pursuit for an adult. Ask those same ten where they've seen martial arts and even a larger majority will say it was on a screen. Sure, there are opportunities we have where we can educate them to some extent. But mass media images are powerful. What we can do, however, is work to counteract stereotypes and the gross parodies of budo demonstrated in popular entertainment.

The e-mail from the public relations fellow caught me on a bad day. I responded, I must admit, a little aggressively. I suggested that demonstrations of any traditional Japanese arts were probably not best secured by referring to them as "services," as if those of us doing them were caterers or prostitutes. I told him that the art I practice has come down through several generations and is over four centuries old, that it is a cultural tradition. I also explained I don't demonstrate it as a way of entertaining but as a means for educating people about Japanese culture in general and the budo specifically. I never heard back from him. That's okay. I don't think a public relations-sponsored party would be the most appropriate theater in which to present any serious martial art. I'm also naïve enough to hope that my reply might have given him a different perspective on budo.

In the case of the university symposium, there wasn't much reply I could make, since I was invited only as a guest. If I had been with the kendo group asked to demonstrate, however, I would have asked to see any promotional materials that were advertising the symposium. Even before that, I would have made it clear that kendo has a history as long and as important as that Meiji era pottery on display. It has a heritage, one with deep roots in Japan, and its principles, like those of all the budo, have had a dramatic and pervasive influence on Japan. Kendo is no less a subject for serious study and demonstration at a program like that the university was mounting than would be the tea ceremony or flower arranging. It *deserves* to be treated with the same respect and consideration as any other art. I would have insisted—politely, but insisted nevertheless—that if kendo was going to be demonstrated at the symposium, that a proper area for the demonstration would be secured. Would you say that "Providing we can find the space, Professor So-&-So will speak?" Huh-uh. The university began planning the program by finding appropriate space for the exhibitions and presentations. Kendo either gets included in that planning or it doesn't get presented at all. At least not by me.

Some would disagree. Any opportunity to present their arts, they would argue, should be taken. Entertainment for kid's birthdays, grand openings of shopping malls; doesn't matter. Any public event should be used to promote their arts, these people would observe. It's a defensible position, I suppose. Maybe you think making the budo popular is more important than making them respectable in the estimation of the general public. Just bear in mind, though, that whichever choice you make when the time comes, the path you take will say something not only about you but about your Way as well.

25

Nitten Soji (Daily Chores)

I began practicing the budo just as I entered high school. Now it is not all that uncommon for an adolescent to count the martial arts among his hobbies or after-school activities. In the sixties when I discovered the budo, however, they were still something of a rarity in the United States. I did not know any other young people my age who were involved in them and I learned to keep my own participation quiet. I'm afraid what most of my classmates knew of the Japanese fighting arts consisted of "karate chops" and "judo throws" as they were depicted in James Bond movies and the like. Admittedly, I would have basked in their thinking I was spending my after-school hours perfecting some arcane and deadly skills. But adolescents being what they are, I was also wise enough to know that some among them would want to see some proof of my "lethal" abilities. That was the sort of attention I did not want. So, having placed my keikogi, my training uniform, in my locker in the morning, when school let out in the afternoon I would tuck it into a bag along with my books. Then I would set off for the dojo in my efforts to acquire an altogether different sort of education than the one afforded me in my high school classes.

I suppose another reason I kept a low key about my practice of the budo was that I derived a certain amount of amusement and satisfaction in knowing that what most people at that time did think of the martial arts was almost cartoonishly inaccurate. Squeezing out the cloth I used to mop the dojo floor with every afternoon, for instance, I would occasionally ask myself "Is this how James Bond got started?"

Before training began properly, you see, it was among my daily chores to attend to the cleaning of the dojo. The dojo itself had been a large dining room in a Victorian era house that my sensei and his wife were renting while they were living in the U.S. Most of the time we practiced outside, in the yard behind the house or at a nearby cemetery. Even when we did, however, I still had to clean the dojo every day. Since I was my sensei's only pupil and since the dojo was relatively spacious, it would have made sense to have used a broom or mop to clean the wooden floor. That method, however, was unacceptable to Sensei. I cleaned the dojo floor the same way they have always been cleaned, the same way floors are cleaned in Buddhist temples and monasteries in Japan.

I filled a bucket with hot water and took a cotton cloth the size of a large dishtowel from a drying line in the basement. These cloths are called *tenugui* in Japanese. They are used in bathing as a combination towel and washcloth. You may buy tenugui in stores in Japan, but most people collect them. Hotels, resorts, businesses; all of these places have their own, personalized tenugui which they distribute as gifts. When they get old and thin and ratty, they are relegated to cleaning rags. I knew every cleaning tenugui we had in the house intimately. My favorite was from a resort, with a printed illustration of a trio of happy monkeys sloshing in a hot spring that was part of the resort. I would do some sloshing myself, swishing the tenugui into the bucket, then squeezing out the excess water. (There was, I was taught when I began my training, a correct way to do even this simple task, and I was not doing it. I would twist the towel held in my two hands, palms down. One day Sensei saw me doing this. He grunted. He turned my hands over, palms up. Years later, when I was in a public bath in Japan for the first time, I noticed immediately that everyone there squeezed out their towels the same way, palms up, the opposite of how it would be done in the West.)

Tenugui in hand, I started at the upper left corner of the dojo. (Actually, I started at the back of the dojo the first time I did it—and learned quickly that that was a mistake as well. "No sweep dirt towards the kamiza!" Sensei shouted, gesturing at the Shinto shrine at the front of the training hall. "Away!") I bent over, legs straight, arms outstretched and I sort of pushed the towel ahead of me, up and down, up and down, in broad strokes the whole length and width of the dojo. It is nearly impossible to perform this task slowly. One's arms are shoving out ahead and the legs fairly scramble to keep up, and so the movement is both breathless and awkward as well as being painful. Then, still panting and with the floor still gleaming and damp, I went on to my other tasks, dusting the kamiza, changing the water in the flower arrangement, and so on. All these chores are a part of training called *nitten soji* in Japanese: daily cleaning.

In a place like a dojo, a place for seeking the Way, there can be no distractions: cleanliness is mandatory. A regular gymnasium may be dusty and dank, but the dojo must be kept aired out and free not only from accumulated grime but even from day-to-day dust. So purely from an aesthetic view, soji is practical and purposeful. It is carried out for that reason, with equal enthusiasm and consistency, in shrines, temples, and monasteries in Japan, just as it is in the martial arts dojo. Then too, there is an intimate connection between the way things are done in the dojo and certain Shinto beliefs. Probably more so than any other religion, Shinto is almost fanatical about cleanliness. Much of its "worship" consists of rituals where the body, or the physical area around one, is cleansed. Sometimes this is in a purely symbolic context, as when a priest purifies with a wand of tree branches or some other special implement. And sometimes the cleaning is cleaning in the real sense of the word. As it is with nitten soji.

The question then, is not whether soji should be done, but rather who should do it? And why? In gyms or health clubs, janitorial services are taken care of by people paid to do them. The instructor at your neighborhood exercise franchise would not likely be spotted sweeping the place up. Asking a paying member to do so would doubtless be met with incredulity, probably even resentment.

Unfortunately, this same attitude prevails at some modern dojo. I visited one karate training hall where soji was being introduced to students for the first time. (I found out later that a student had joined this dojo not long before, one who had done some training in Japan and who had asked his new teacher why the floors were not cleaned before and after class as they were in Japanese dojo. In embarrassment, I imagine, the teacher instituted soji.) To my considerable surprise, the teacher announced that the cleaning activities before and after class would be performed by the junior students and that the teacher and his senior students would be excused from it. I suppose the teacher thought the humble task of soji beneath him and his advanced pupils. Or perhaps he wished to make the senior students feel special and to give the more junior members of the dojo something to work towards, to stick it out long enough to be excused from cleaning chores. Soji, however, is not a signature of status. I have been to other dojo, I am happy to say, where even very highly ranked teachers got out on the floor after conducting training, cleaning cloth in hand, to work side by side with the freshest beginner at daily chores. This is the true spirit of the budo.

During my early training years I suffered through the usual throes of awkwardness and the social and personal anxieties of most teenagers. Sometimes it was tempting to carry the frustrations of the day into my training in the evening, dividing my attention and detracting from practice. What kept me from doing that was the mechanics of soji. Filling the bucket, squeezing out the cloth, and swooping up and down the shadowy, empty dojo floor, my mind was gradually swept clear of the incidents of the day. While I might have begun my chores tired, angry, or dejected, by the end of soji, I invariably felt better.

The budoka who undertakes soji as part of his daily training absorbs himself into it. It is mundane and humbling, but somehow it elevates the spirit and it reminds us that no matter what the level of our skills, a fundamental necessity of budo is the incessant scouring away of that which is superfluous, dusting off the detritus accumulating on our minds. We finish our daily chores at the dojo with a training hall that is clean and neat and at the same time, we gain even more. Soji may not be the most efficient way of cleaning a dojo. But it is a wonderful method of polishing the spirit.

26

A Dash of Yellow *Eba*

I don't know much about Nigerian cooking.

That's a lie, actually. Actually, I know absolutely *nothing* about Nigerian cooking. If I wanted to learn, if you were skilled at the cuisine and wished to teach me, I'd probably be a reasonably good student. Why? Well, for the simple reason I would not bring to my lessons any preconceived notions. When you were explaining the basics of pounding *iyan* yam, I would not be thinking, "Oh, yeah, that's the way I saw it done in that movie about the cooking of Nigeria." When you were explaining the proper way to mix *eba* flour into stock for *ogbono* soup you would not have to worry that I was being distracted by thoughts of "Wait a minute, that's not the way Smythe said it was done in his three-volume series on the cooking of Nigeria I've read five times." I've never seen any movies on the cooking of Nigeria. Or read any books about it. I am a blank slate on the subject. I am ready for you to fill in the information.

The average person interested in the traditional Japanese martial arts, the koryu or "old schools," really doesn't know much about them. He does not understand their structure, the means by which they are propagated. That's okay. The koryu are an obscure subject to be sure. What isn't okay is that the average person does not recognize his lack of knowledge. Quite the opposite. He is, in many cases, convinced he does know quite a bit about the subject. Sometimes, though he doesn't think of it in this way, he may actually believe he knows more than a teacher. Given the paucity of koryu even in Japan, never mind its rarity in the West, the knowledge this average person has acquired is almost never through personal exposure to the classical martial arts of old Japan.

In addition to the sources provided by movies, books, and questionable examples, the prospective student of a koryu bases his "knowledge" about the classical martial arts on what he already knows about the modern budo: karate-do, aikido, judo, and so on. He assumes koryu are organized and taught the same way. He may be very disappointed when he doesn't see a koryu training session where students are lined up neatly in rows going through movements. He may suspect it really isn't a martial art at all because no one is shouting "*Osu!*" Or because no one bows to the teacher after the teacher gives some instruction. He is accustomed to these rituals in the modern budo dojo and assumes they are universal in all Japanese martial disciplines. These arts do not meet his expectations and rather than considering the possibility those expectations might be misplaced or in error, he can become frustrated.

On a regular basis, I am asked to explain and narrate chado, the tea ceremony of Japan. I explain the movements as they unfold, also giving a history of chado and trying to convey a sense of its goals and philosophies. It's enjoyable but challenging. The biggest obstacle I face is not the relative ignorance most Westerners have about chado. No, my biggest headache is exactly the one I just described about koryu. We get people who *think* they know what chado is. "This is a sacred ritual!" one woman hissed at me after the conclusion of a tea ceremony I narrated. She was so angry at what she perceived as a tone of flippancy on my part during my narration that she was literally shaking. I listened to her tirade, then asked her if she practiced chado. "No," she fumed, "but I've read *a lot* about it!" Her response was perfect. Exactly the sort of attitude we see all too often regarding koryu from some people. They haven't any firsthand knowledge or experience. But they've read *a lot* of books. And they "know."

I can tell you that this problem of preconceived notions is among the most troublesome of those faced by exponents who are trying to teach koryu outside Japan. Nearly as big a problem is the Mistaken Assumption. A while back, on an Internet forum, the subject of tattoos came up. Specifically, a correspondent wished to know if having a tattoo would have any repercussions in training in a koryu or being accepted into one. A very senior exponent replied that he would not allow a student to begin training with him if the student sported that sort of body art. The immediate barrage of outrage over this rivaled the London Blitz. The teacher was accused of being "Victorian" for his prudery. Of being a Philistine for his inability to recognize tattooing as a form of artistic expression. Of being a troglodyte for being insensitive. It went on and on. Of all those protesting, none had even a fraction of the experience of this teacher. Yet what struck me was that none of them asked *why* the teacher had such a policy.

Remember when I said above that some people think they know more about koryu than the koryu teacher? The tattoo issue is a perfect example. Those disagreeing with the authority's response mistakenly assumed koryu had to meet the same standards as other conventions in our world. That they must be democratic, open to all, tolerant of individual tastes and needs. They have to be "fair." Instead of using the opportunity to question the authority and find out more about why someone of his vast experience and expertise had reached such a conclusion, they hammered away with their mistaken assumptions.

No one enjoys being told they don't know what they're talking about. Even if we suspect it's true, we resent having it pushed in our face. Even more so, when we have devoted some time to reading and talking with others, we hate thinking that such efforts may have been wasted or are not worth so much as we thought. The next time, though, that you are tempted to become angry when your preconceived notions and possibly mistaken assumptions are held up to you, think about Nigerian cooking, please. Think less about the irritation at having your ideas attacked and more about the opportunity to expose yourself to new and wider experiences. It isn't always pleasant. It may even be something you don't want to hear. Trust me, though. It's the best way to begin learning to cook.

27

Death by Appointment

There is one bit of karate esoterica which has never particularly appealed to me as a training goal, I must admit. Yet it is one which is fascinating, nonetheless. It is the arcane skill known by names like *sannen goroshi* or *gotsuki goroshi*, the science of dispatching an opponent with a blow not immediately fatal upon contact, but which works its deadly magic in three years (*sannen*) or five months (*gotsuki*) or some other specifically stated period of time. Collectively, this mystical power is known in Japanese as *okurasu goroshi*, literally "delayed killing."

Stories of the Chinese martial arts are the most fertile ground for these accounts of delayed death. As an occult relative to the more pedestrian arts of *tien hsueh* or "striking at vital points," the art of inflicting a wound that would in time prove to be fatal is one said to have been perfected by many kung fu adepts. Some of those possessing these skills, the tales from China have it, did not even need to strike their adversaries with any great physical force; simply a light touch was enough to do the trick.

Several explanations have been advanced to explain the mysterious power of these strikes with their postponed effects. According to Chinese philosophies and theories, channels of energy, chi, or, in Japanese, ki, flow through the body at regular intervals and when manipulated correctly the resultant imbalance in the flow results in death at a later date or time that is predictable. Other authorities of various reputations (there is no lack of opinions or those offering them on this subject) insist it is not so much the vital point being struck that's important, but the *way* in which it is attacked. They cite the concussive vibrations inflicted by karate and kung fu blows as the real power behind the art, attacks which may do little damage at the surface, but devastate internally. Still others scoff at the whole notion, and attribute a voodoo-like power of suggestion to the morbid effects of the delayed death.

Japanese and Okinawan karate tales lack the macabre and spectacular claims of the more fabulous stories of the delayed death touch in Chinese lore. Even so, karate has an abundance of such reputed incidents. I once put the question of their veracity to my two karate sensei, who had been born and raised on Okinawa. Both were reasonably pragmatic men; both had graduate degrees in economics, and neither put too much stock in ancient superstitions. Yet both men expressed a belief in okurasu goroshi. One of them gave me an example of it that he had heard while a child on Okinawa, and he gave me a possible explanation. I pass them along for you to consider.

Near Yonabaru village in Okinawa was a karateman named Kaneshiro who was reputed to possess the skills of okurasu goroshi, although he had never put them into actual practice. It was in the closing months of the Second World War, when Kaneshiro was forced to utilize the art. He was working in the sweet potato patch of a neighbor when a Japanese soldier stationed on Okinawa came by and demanded money. The soldier had been dispatched on some errand for his captain. But he was a drunkard and had gotten sidetracked when he came across a group of Okinawans sharing a jug of *awamori*. The soldier had joined them and had chugged more than his share of this amazingly potent brew. Afterwards, he had gotten lost in the countryside and had ended up threatening the wrong farmer. Kaneshiro broke the soldier's wrist and then struck him. The strike, done with the edge of Kaneshiro's hand, knocked the wind out of the soldier, who was at the time obviously much more concerned with the pain of the broken wrist. As for Kaneshiro, he knew that such an assault would be grounds for his execution immediately by the Japanese army. He fled into the jungle, but before he left, he warned the soldier that the man had only three days to live. The soldier returned to his unit, yet sure enough, three days later he fell ill and died. Blood poisoning was given as the cause.

The battle for Okinawa began not long after this incident. The Japanese forces there had more to worry about than hunting down Kaneshiro. And not long after that, of course, the war ended. For decades afterward, Kaneshiro's feat was repeated often enough to become the stuff of legend in that part of Okinawa, and he was much sought after as a karate teacher. He consistently refused to divulge the essentials of his abilities, however. It was not until a few weeks before his own death, several years later, when he spoke about it to one of his students.

"The strike I used was one done with the tegatana (knife hand)," he said, "and I aimed it one handspan above the liver." And one more thing, he added.

"I guessed from the looks of him that he was quite a heavy drinker." That is all Kaneshiro would reveal. He would not, or maybe could not, explain why this particular strike had the effect it did. The student he told, though, passed the information down to other students, and one who'd gained knowledge of these deaths took the information to a physician.

Based upon the information he was given, the doctor noted that "the strike indicated was with the edge of the hand, which makes more contact with a larger area of the target than would, say, a punch." And, the doctor said, "Kaneshiro's target was precisely at the level of the spleen." The attack could have smashed the spleen, the doctor theorized, an organ that, among other functions, helps regulate the supply of blood. He added that it would take about a week in an otherwise healthy adult for the infection of the ruptured spleen to have spread enough to have caused death. For an alcoholic whose spleen had been damaged by long-term heavy drinking? Death would be much faster. In about three days.

In this instance, perhaps a scientific explanation can account for the mystery behind the okurasu goroshi. Even so, it cannot answer all our questions: How, for instance could Kaneshiro have known of the effects of a spleen infection in the first place? The soldier was drunk at the time, but how did Hiro know his opponent was a habitual drinker whose spleen would have been especially vulnerable? And how did he control his strike to do just the needed damage and no more? Maybe the answer lies in further scientific investigation. But maybe all the answers lie in the grave of a karateman from Yonabaru village.

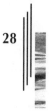

28

White Boys & Bonsai

Last autumn, the Humanities department of a college in Washington began compiling material for a symposium they planned on the experiences of *nisei* and *sansei* (second- and third-generation Japanese-Americans). I was contacted by a graduate student working on the program, who asked me for a short written contribution about my own experiences.

I was a trifle confused. I was afraid the graduate student was a bit confused as well. Simply put, I am not of Japanese ancestry, not by any stretch of the imagination. I told her this, explaining that my primary connection with things Japanese had to do with my training in the martial Ways and my writing about Japanese culture. She knew all that, she replied. But my name had been suggested by a nisei English professor who had read some of my writing. And while there would be no other contributors of non-Japanese ancestry in the symposium, she hoped I would be interested in participating.

To be invited to contribute to a project of this kind had me more than interested. I appreciated the recognition and the opportunity. But there was one problem. I hadn't the slightest idea what to write about. I had nearly a year before the submission was due, time enough to give me some afternoons to think about it, to remember my own experiences and observations. And it wasn't long until I was reminded of the sermon of Nishimoto sensei, on the subject of white boys and bonsai.

Nishimoto sensei was an osho, a priest of the Jodo sect of Buddhism, from Colorado. He was also a fifth dan in judo, who served frequently as a referee at the shiai, or tournaments we held in the Midwest when I was a young judoka. His shaven head and short, stocky frame were a familiar sight at shiai and despite his gentle disposition, he was respected as a formidable expert in judo and a strict disciplinarian. I remember being in the dressing room once after a shiai when Garry Matsukawa came in, angry and frustrated. Garry had lost two matches that, given his abilities, he should easily have won. He took out some of his irritation on a locker door that had been left ajar, whacking it loudly with the palm of his hand as he passed by. Nishimoto sensei was walking in behind Garry and he saw it. *Wham!* Garry was grabbed by the back of his collar and sat down on the gym bench, sat down so hard his eyes kind of rattled about in their sockets for a few seconds. He worked on regaining his senses while Nishimoto proceeded to deliver to him a lecture explaining the importance of self-control in judo, on and off the mats. A lecture delivered in no uncertain terms, terms quite clear even to a thirteen-year-old like Garry. Even though he was a Buddhist clergyman, that is the sort of man Nishimoto was. I suppose that is why the other judo sensei called on him to straighten out the matter of the white boy problem.

At that time you see, back in the late sixties, judo and all the other martial Ways were divided in a sense. On one side were "the real kind" or, as they preferred it in pidgin shorthand "dakine." On the other side were "the white boys." Dakine were almost all nisei and sansei. They usually spoke Japanese or pidgin English among themselves. They took pride in the fact that they practiced a wholly traditional kind of judo and upheld its ideals. Dakine could kneel in the posture of seiza for an hour at a judo shiai without moving or fidgeting at all, then jump to their feet when their names were called and enter a match at full tilt. Dakine held in disdain anyone who showed much emotion at winning or losing. They believed in doing things the old way—the samurai way, as they thought of it. And very simply they considered any judoka who held different views to be a "white boy."

Now, I must hasten to add that the derisive label of white boy had no racial significance. Blacks, Caucasians, even others of Japanese ancestry; I heard kids of every background called a white boy. It had little to do with their race; much more to do with their inability or refusal to hold the old ways of doing things in the same high regard as dakine. They were, for that reason, beneath contempt. Conversely, there were a few of us not of Japanese ancestry who had also been brought up with the same ideas by our sensei, and while our skin may have been as white as the bleached judogi we wore or dark as a new black belt, we were considered every bit as much dakine as any Kato, Tanaka, or Suzuki.

Among ourselves, we all used versions of the same sorts of demeaning nicknames most young people do with one another. A dakine could stand being teased by being called a *jimbei* or a *bonkura*, both Japanese slang words for "idiot" or "hillbilly." But the worst insult, one a dakine never used to another, not even in joking, not even in fun, was to call another dakine a white boy. It would only be fair to note too, that for all their arrogance and cliquishness, dakine were not, by typical Western standards, examples of machismo. Bob Miyoshi, one of dakine, was a member of a group training in the distinctly un-macho art of classical Japanese dance. Garry Matsukawa played the *shakuhachi* bamboo flute. Nor could dakine be categorized as un-American. All had been born in this country, and as far as I could tell by their attitudes, all were loyal to it and did not consider themselves markedly different from other kids with whom they went to school and played and hung out with. They—our—egalitarianism might have resembled that of a college fraternity, yet neither money nor popularity earned a place in the circle of dakine. To be dakine came only with a willingness to pursue judo or the other budo with a very traditional Japanese approach. That was the yardstick. Meet it and you could consider yourself a member.

Nevertheless, even though the appellation of white boy was not racially motivated, it was causing some trouble, especially when a lot of us got together at judo shiai. Dakine dressed in a different part of the locker room. During matches, you would hear the usual "Come on!" or "Give 'em!", but also, muttered and taunting, "Come on, come on, white boy."

Our various sensei knew where this was leading, and so Nishimoto was selected by them to put an end to it. It happened while we were in the changing room, putting on our judogi for a tournament at the University of Oklahoma. Nishimoto sensei came into the room and began pointing here and there, motioning for some of us in the crowd to follow him. It was an uncomfortable moment. I turned away from his selection process and took a sudden and intense interest in examining my lapels.

"*Oi! Kimi!*" I heard, and I turned to see him beckoning to me. I joined the rest of those he picked out, going slowly into a small trainer's room down the hall.

"Boys," Nishimoto sensei addressed us as we sat quietly, in various states of dress. "You're all *nikkeijin*, aren't you?"

"Yo," thought I. My exit line. Sensei had made a mistake. "Nikkejin" refers to anyone whose ancestry is Japanese and so I was sidling out the door. I was by no means the only non-Japanese among dakine, but I was the only one who'd been summoned to attendance at this little convention. "Sit back down," Sensei said. I sat.

"You are all nikkeijin," he went on. "But that doesn't mean you are all Japanese." Nishimoto sensei paused and folded his arms across his broad chest. Most of dakine were looking puzzled. "Some of you have been to my church in Denver," he went on. "You know the bonsai I have out in the yard there?" A few heads nodded. Nishimoto sensei cultivated Ezo spruce trees, keeping them in pots. They were twisted and gnarled with age, even though the largest of them was scarcely as tall as my waist. "We don't have Ezo spruce in this country," he went on. "The ones I have were imported when they were just seedlings, from Japan. But that was seventy years ago. All the training and wiring I've done on those trees, all the repotting and fertilizing and care; everything that's made the trees what they are today, that was done in America. So tell me boys: are those trees Japanese or American?"

I looked at Rick Funai, sitting beside me. He was looking at the floor. On my other side, Bob Miyoshi rubbed his chin. No one said anything. "Well, let me ask you another question," Sensei went on. "If that spruce had been brought from Japan and just planted, just left here to grow naturally, would it be anything special right now?"

"No Sensei," offered Bob. "It would be just another tree."

"Yes," agreed Nishimoto sensei. "You know, Miyoshi-san, you're like that tree. You've got roots in Japan. But unless you train yourself to make something worthwhile grow out of those roots, what's their value? You'll be just another tree."

That was the end of the sermon. Nishimoto sensei had not said a word about the white boys thing. Instead, his message was about our way of thinking. Sitting properly in seiza, like the other refinements judo had taught us, were accomplishments of which to be proud. But they were not an end in themselves. It was, Sensei was trying to tell us, how we used that tradition and discipline that would set us apart, make us special.

Those of us with roots in Japan, whether they are roots of blood or of the lineage of our Ways, take pride in the connection. We have strong roots. That is what I wrote about for the symposium on the social experiences of Japanese-Americans. I suppose that is one of the lessons that my own experiences with that group have taught me, to be aware of roots. And to remember that the important thing is what grows from them.

29

Ai-Uchi (Mutual Striking)

Not that anyone is likely to ask me. . . . But in the doubtful instance my opinion was sought in improving the level of competition in those forms of the modern budo that have it, I would reply simply with this advice: I would reassign with the importance it once had to the classical warrior of old Japan, the concept of *ai-uchi*.

Ai-uchi is Japanese for, literally, "mutual striking." It is specifically a term used in the martial arts, referring to those moments when combatants deliver blows simultaneously, or so nearly so that the referees and judges are unable to render a decision. The rules of kendo competition have provisions for ai-uchi, as does karate, and *naginata-do*, the modern form of using the naginata or halberd. In the formal contests for each of these, an ai-uchi is ignored in the scoring. The referee crosses the red and white flags he holds to announce the mutual strikes and no point or penalty is awarded for either contestant.

Ai-uchi meant something entirely different for the samurai on the battlefield in old Japan. For him, mutual striking was the only possible outcome of a fight with an opponent of equal skills, and it was the only result he could hope for when coming into a match against an enemy of superior ability.

My sensei once explained this very convincingly for me in his own way. He was at the dining room table one afternoon when I came by, practicing *shodo*, the Way of calligraphy. He was very accomplished as a calligrapher; his brush-strokes were exactly like his movements with the sword. His writing was decisive and bold and very correct, the strokes brushed with balance and a kind of elegance. While I watched him, he took a clean sheet of paper and dipped and rolled his brush in the well of the inkstone, turning it over until he had a sharp wet point with the bristles. He wrote "Thirty-three and one-third percent" on the paper, using Japanese numerals that I had recently learned to read, and gave it to me. Since he had just been working on some beautiful poetry, I wondered what this was all about.

"That is the attitude for entering a fight," he said.

"Thirty-three and a third percent?"

"Those are your chances for survival when you fight a battle to the death," he said. There is a one-third chance that you will be better than your opponent, more skilled or experienced or braver or luckier. In that case, you will kill him and escape unharmed yourself. There is a one-third chance that he will be better than you in any of those areas, meaning that he will kill you and be unhurt himself. (In truth, in a situation where the samurai faced a superior enemy, mutual death was also likely to take place because the warrior could not achieve his aim—destroying the opponent—except by exposing himself to a fatal counterstroke in the process. He sacrificed himself deliberately.) And the final one-third chance will be that you and your enemy will be close to equal in terms of skill or luck or spirit. And in that case you will both die. One-third of a chance of surviving a battle. It was something for me to think about and something which, for me, put ai-uchi into perspective.

Of course, modern shiai or budo competition is not a matter of life and death. It is, at best, a not-terribly-effective adjunct to daily training. It can have the effect of putting the budoka under stress, forcing him to conduct himself well under difficult and unusual circumstances. It can challenge his ego, force him to face his fears, and teach him to have confidence in his abilities. At its worst, competition in the budo frequently gives way to wild and unrestrained efforts to "score," even when such scoring has little relation to an actual combative situation. Kendo, karate, and naginata-do all suffer from this problem. In each of these disciplines, exponents in a competitive situation often give in to the temptation to whale away with abandon, striking out indiscriminately and heedless of the countering strikes that result in the call of ai-uchi. And why not? One can hardly blame the competitor. If their strike reaches their opponent slightly before his hits them, they may gain a point. At best, they will connect at the same time, usually nullifying their efforts. Sporting competition had made ai-uchi a viable form of strategy.

If the change in scoring that I am suggesting were instituted, though, that kind of thinking would very likely change. What would happen to the strategy of the competitor, for instance, if a call of ai-uchi during a contest resulted in the immediate disqualification of both contestants? What would the results be if ai-uchi were scored the same way as a *hikiwake* (a draw or tie), which is interpreted as a loss for both?

I think this revision in the rules might signal a different attitude in competition, one more in keeping with the mentality of the samurai going into battle rather than that of the sports enthusiast entering a tournament. The budoka facing an opponent in a formal contest might be more inclined to employ correct body shifting, maneuvering for position; being absolutely sure before launching an attack. Strikes would have to be clean and quick and doubtless fewer in number. The emphasis would be on *ikken hisatsu*, the "one strike decides all" kind of strategy that is inherent in the philosophy of the budo. Knowing that a call of ai-uchi will be a loss in a contest, the budoka might also strive to improve his defensive skills. He would not be able to afford to cut loose with a feeble counter when an attack came; he would either commit himself totally to a responding attack that would score before his opponent could, or he would be forced to parry and shift.

On the other hand, maybe I am overemphasizing the importance of ai-uchi. Those forms of the budo which have instituted competition have already moved very far away from the spirit of the battlefield. A sport is not a matter of life and death and it cannot be. A budo that emphasizes the winning of tournaments and competition under all sorts of rules has seriously compromised itself as a martial Way. But if the budoka is, even in a distant and fragmented way, an inheritor of the warrior tradition of old Japan, he should at least do some thinking about what ai-uchi and its consequences meant for that samurai. Those consequences were far more serious, today's budoka must understand, than a referee's crossed flags.

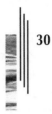

30

Musubi Dachi (Preparatory Stance)

"Perfection is attained through an attention to details."
—Michelangelo

A karateka I know who had just completed six months of training in Japan was telling me about the experience. His principal reason for going to Japan was to gain some instruction in the more advanced meanings of the movements of the kata. He presented a *shokai*, a letter of introduction signed by his teacher, to the secretary at the dojo in Tokyo, and it so happened, the secretary told him, that he had arrived just in time for a class composed of black belts who were studying one of the more difficult kata. Shaking aside his jet lag and the sense of unreality that all budoka have when they come to Japan for the first time, my friend dressed for training and lined up with the rest of the group on the dojo floor.

There was a quick warm-up, then my friend was introduced, and practice began. He moved through the kata with the rest of the class, watching them from the corner of his eye. He was, as it has always been when foreign budoka train in a Japanese dojo for the first time, both surprised and disappointed when the floor did not tremble when the Japanese punched and kicked, when they looked, in fact, pretty much like the karateka with whom he trained back home. The class was separated into smaller groups, each led by a more senior black belt. My friend was delighted when the teacher took him aside alone and asked him to demonstrate the kata.

"I bowed to begin the kata," he said, "then I stepped out into the yoi (beginning) position."

"No, try again," the teacher said.

My friend was confused, but he bowed again and once more he stepped out into the yoi position.

"No, that is wrong," the teacher repeated.

"How could I be wrong," my friend said he was wondering, "when I hadn't done anything yet."

As it turned out, my friend was making a common error in karate practice. When bowing at the start of the kata he placed his feet both pointing forward, touching side by side. This was understandable, he explained, since the command given in English at his Stateside dojo just before the order to bow was "Feet together!" Naturally, my friend and many other budoka bring their feet into a parallel position when they bow.

In the Japanese dojo, he was corrected and shown the proper way to situate one's feet while bowing. This involves placing the heels together, with the toes pointing out at about a 45° angle. What my friend learned was the fundamental difference between *heisoku dachi* ("feet-together stance" is the best translation I can manage), and *musubi dachi* ("preparatory stance").

Considering the myriad details the karateka must contend with during the practice of kata, it at first appears more than a little picky to be worried about which way one's feet are pointing while bowing. It seems, in fact, utterly trivial in comparison to learning the correct methods of striking with the fist or blocking with one's forearm. However, it may prove beneficial for the karateka who feels this way to arrange a brief test, enlisting the aid of a pushy friend. And I might add that while we are talking specifically about the discipline of karate here, musubi dachi occurs in all of the martial Ways. It occurs as well in art like Japanese dance and Kabuki and Noh theater and it has the same significance in each of them.

With your friend standing beside you, assume heisoku dachi. This is the stance my friend took before he was corrected. The feet in heisoku dachi are pressed together along their length in this stance, parallel to one another. Now, in heisoku dachi, slowly execute a bow. Instruct your friend to gently push you sometime during the salutation. Feet together, balance reduced to a minimum, you will be easily toppled. Repeat the same test, but this time place your feet as they should be in musubi dachi. They will touch at the heels, turned out on that 45° plane I mentioned before. In musubi dachi, you will discover both that your posture is more stable and that you are readily able to move with or into the direction of the push, to effectively defend against it.

Heisoku dachi, the parallel-feet stance, does occur at various places in several karate kata, but its meaning and application are different. The purpose of musubi dachi is to establish a feeling of awareness, an on-guard stability that offers protection from several directions at once. For the same reason, the standing bows that are performed in the budo, in greeting or acknowledgment or at the end or beginning of a kata, are always done in the same stance, musubi dachi, always ready for an attack.

There is, though, a deeper meaning still to the stance of musubi dachi. The word *musubi* has more than one connotation. It is usually written with characters that mean "to conclude" or "to close." But it can be written as well to mean "numberless," or "infinite." This is a good way to think of musubi dachi. Musubi, in this instance, carries with it the connotation of "infinite possibilities." When the karateka bows and straightens in musubi dachi, he stands ready to move in a virtually uncountable number of directions. Depending upon the dictates of the particular kata, his actions may develop in a wide variety of ways, all proceeding from the nucleus of musubi dachi. The karateka is the originator of his own movements, and it is the germination of musubi dachi that allows them to flow smoothly and with perfect spontaneity. Approached this way, the importance of the beginning stance becomes obvious. If it is not correct, then no matter how polished one's attacks and defenses, they will be useless.

In aikido, we find the term *kimusubi*, which refers to the linking (musubi, in this case written to mean "knotting together") or creative joining of two spirits (ki). An opponent punches, and is blocked by your own arm; in the process, energy is created. The word for this moment of creation is musubi, the fertile point from which all further action springs. Will it be necessary to counterattack and prevent the opponent from attempting to harm you further, or will the simple misdirection of his attack be enough to stop him? Whatever the response, it will arise through musubi.

There are times, in my own pursuit of the budo, when I feel as though the details of these arts are like the stray ends of a huge ball of string. Take one at random, tug on it, and you will begin to unravel the whole ball. Musubi dachi is one of those details. Outwardly, it looks so ordinary that most untrained people would not recognize it at all, dismiss it merely as a person standing. Only when one begins to explore it, to look beneath its surface, to pull on the string, does he start to discover inner meanings. Like most of what is extraordinary about the budo, musubi dachi is superficially ordinary. We must never, though, take these details for granted. Look below the surface. Pull on the strings. That is the only way to unravel the mysteries of the Way.

31

Hacho (Deliberate Asymmetry)

I was in the backwoods of central Japan, high up in the mountains, visiting a small town called Narai. Narai is quite a special place. It dates back far into the feudal period, when it was famous for its woodworking products. The giant pines and other trees that grew in the Kiso Valley where Narai is, were so luxuriant and huge that the area was known to the shogun who ruled Japan as a source of fine wood. By a decree from the first of the Tokugawa shogun, Tokugawa Ieyasu, all the trees around Narai belonged to him. Not a single one could be cut without official sanctions.

In the modernization that swept Japan after the Second World War, Narai was missed. To be honest, Narai got missed the first time Japan modernized, late in the 19th century. It is a little village tucked at the foot of the mountains. If you squint your eyes just a bit, it looks exactly as it did in the 1700s. Narai is a haven for traditional artists and folk crafts. I wandered through the narrow streets, looking at magnificently carved wooden tables and other works of folk art that had prices ten times what I paid for my house. I was staggered at the prices. But I was almost as surprised when, looking into a small woodworking shop, I saw a carpenter using a *sumi tsubo*.

When a carpenter in the West needs a straight line, he depends upon a snapped chalk line. When he wants a curve, he uses a template to give him a precise, geometrically precise curve. When the Japanese carpenter needs a line he also relies on something like a chalk line, a sumi tsubo. This is a carved piece of wood roughly the size and shape of a bar of soap. It has a well that is stuffed with ink-impregnated cotton, and a line of string that can be wound out and back. The string passes through the inked cotton and is drawn out so it can be snapped down to leave a guideline on wood that is to be cut. I discovered in talking with the carpenter that sumi tsubo are not all that unusual; they are still used by many workmen in Japan. Had he ever used a Western chalk string I asked him. He reluctantly admitted that he had. He didn't want to hurt my feelings, he said, but he thought the sumi tsubo was superior to the Western version.

"After all," he said, "you can't lay a curved line with a chalk string." I was intrigued. Could you do that with a sumi tsubo? "Sure," he said, and he showed me. He plucked the line just as he snapped it, twisting the cord to make it curve.

As you might guess, quivering the line with a twitch of the fingers is not the most exact method of getting a geometrically accurate curve. Sometimes in a Japanese home built with such traditional techniques, in fact, you can see the imperfection of the curves in lintels, transoms, and so on. It is not that the Japanese are sloppy builders; it is because Japanese culture has a special affinity with *hacho*: "deliberate asymmetry."

Anyone who has had the exact position of every part of his body meticulously, endlessly corrected by a budo sensei will doubt the notion of the Japanese being loose and flexible in their approach to anything traditional. A teacher will adjust the angle of your shoulders to within what seems like centimeters before he is satisfied with your posture, or move your chin back and forth like a metronome until he gets the carriage of your head just right. There seem to be some ideal dimensions and lines out there, the budoka often thinks, ones that he cannot see but which the sensei is measuring him against. Still, as he gains experience and visits other dojo, the budoka may notice variations, slight differences in the way different teachers will go about teaching or performing the same things.

The art of karate is a good example here. I do not mean differences between styles of the art—the distinctions say, between the Goju ryu and the Shito ryu. I am referring to variations, particularly in the kata, in the teachings of different sensei within a single school or style. In the Japan Karate Association, for instance, one sensei will have his students leaping forward at a certain part of a kata, while another will teach his students to slide. In another kata a movement will be slow and deliberate in one dojo, fast and snappy in another.

These apparent inconsistencies drive some budoka crazy. They imagine fervently that there is one "right" way to do a kata, a standard that has been set sometime in the hazy past, to which all students must aspire. Unfortunately, some teachers may exploit this idea. They will insist that theirs is the "correct" method of the kata and hint broadly that other teachers are not following the path set by the founder of the art. Others use budo organizations to codify a standard way of performing the kata. I call this unfortunate because it is incon-sistent with the spirit of the budo.

Karate is a good example to use here, but practitioners of any of the modern budo will recognize the problem. Most modern styles of Japanese karate began with a single founder who had a core of original students. These students or their students in turn are today the senior teachers. As they spread out over Japan and later the world, these disciples tended consciously in some cases and unconsciously in others, to imbue their own personalities into their karate. Perhaps one of them had long legs, and so found, in that kata I mentioned earlier, they could move more effectively by sliding. Maybe the founder of the system taught it originally with the slide, but emphasized a stamping action to one of his students for some reason. The student kept it in the kata and passed it on to his students who now practice and teach the stamping variation as gospel.

(You would be surprised at the "orthodox" way of doing techniques that have their origin in some personal quirk of a past master. In one ryu devoted to the art of the stick, an unusually short headmaster had a habit of banging the end of the stick on the ground during a certain point in some kata. It had nothing to do with the technique; he was merely too short. Two generations later, his stick-banging is now considered a fundamental point in those kata.)

In Japan, despite the image many budo organizations like to give of complete standardization, there is actually tolerance for a whole range of "correct" ways to do the kata and other techniques. That is not to suggest that anything goes. But it is obvious watching the same kata performed by senior practitioners of the same system in Japan who come from different regions of the country, that there is no single exact way of interpreting them.

Naturally, in the West, the same is true. The difference between Japan and the Occident, however, is that here, many times students are made to feel smug or stupid if their kata is varied from others in the same style. That is too bad. Because karate kata, like all the kata and methods of the budo, are subject to a certain amount of hacho—deliberate asymmetry. There is nothing wrong with the kata of a karateka from Michigan looking slightly different at points than the same one performed by a practitioner from New Mexico. Not so long as both are training under qualified sensei and both have an understanding of the movements they are performing.

Keep in mind the asymmetry of hacho the next time you hear budoka squabbling about whether this or that rendition of a kata is the "right" one. And when you see a kata or a technique demonstrated in a way different from what you were taught, remember that it is not a sign that something is wrong with that person's budo training, or with yours. It is simply a natural expression of the art. It is budo's version of hacho.

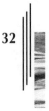

32

The Strike and the Thrust

The karateka must grasp the distinctions, in his arsenal of weapons, between attacks that are *thrusting* in nature and those which are *striking* attacks. To the novice, the differences will be invisible. They are too subtle for him to grasp. As he progresses, he will begin to appreciate them. The senior karateka will not only recognize the varied body mechanics that separate striking and thrusting, he will employ them unconsciously, to maximum efficiency.

A thrusting technique is probably the first offensive movement you learned in the karate dojo: the *choku zuki* or "straight punch." (Note that *zuki* here is the compound form of *tsuki*.) *Tsuki waza*, or thrusting techniques, involve force driven out in a single straight line. With the straight punch, the fist is cocked at the side, then pushed forward in a twisting corkscrew motion so that at the moment it reaches the target the arm is extended, the elbow very nearly but not entirely locked.

As his training continues, the karateka begins to perceive some distinctions. He can feel the reciprocal action of karate's tsuki waza, the principle that makes them so powerful. This entails a precise attention to the *hikite*, the "withdrawing hand" that is retracted in a push-pull motion, as the thrusting hand goes out. The more forcefully he pulls back, the more power the karateka imparts in shooting out the punch. For the most part, the karateka at this level will accomplish all this through rotation of his shoulders. Only with much more practice will he relax to the point where he can sink his rotational movement down into his hips.

The intermediate karateka will also learn that the corkscrew motion that characterizes thrusting is not so simple. While the beginner rotates his fist beginning at the start of the punch, the advanced practitioner makes this action only the last few inches before contact, greatly amplifying the torque of the attack.

The very advanced karateka will discover finally that the thrust is anything but a simple straight line. In fact, the thrust of the expert expands and contracts at contact, in such a way that staggering shock waves are imparted to the target. It was a mastery of this force of physics that allowed Okinawan karate greats of the past to thrust a punch out that actually drew the opponent in when it contacted and caused him to fall face down.

Striking techniques, for the beginner, seem far more complex than thrusting. Rather than relying on a single, linear thrust, *uchi waza* (striking techniques) depend upon an arcing motion. The *soto uraken uchi*, or "outer backfist strike" is a good example. There is a reciprocal action in the movement. But instead of push-pull, the arms cross over, the strike coming laterally from below. The power of this strike is delivered in a whipping swing, the elbow a fulcrum.

Beginners will do well just to get the gross movement of striking down. Intermediate practitioners will occupy themselves with a host of details. The lateral rotation of the fist coming around from horizontal to vertical must be polished. Attention must be given to the flexibility of the elbow throughout the motion to maximize speed, as well as to the crucially important contraction of the shoulder muscles to provide stability. All of these contribute to a snapping kind of force, a whipcrack.

It takes at least a few years before any kind of proficiency in uchi waza is attained. The factors are too complex, the angles too diverse. Unfortunately, once a basic technical proficiency is gained in striking, many karateka cease to study, settling instead to repeat their uchi waza at the same level. They may strive to increase their speed and succeed fractionally. But rarely will they be able to increase the power of their strikes. Creating more power in striking actions in karate practice can come only through the guidance of a skilled sensei who will teach the student to relax his shoulders and to properly generate rotational power from the hips.

Watch the strikes at a typical karate tournament sometime. Even if they connected, they would only stun, perhaps. They would sting like a boxer's jab, nothing more. In fact, the karateka may eventually decide that to be the real purpose of uchi waza. Unless he is lucky enough to see the killing power inherent in the strikes of a true expert in the art, he may never know just how wrong he is.

The strength of thrusts is in their devastating force. Their weakness is that with the limb extended, they make it susceptible to being seized and locked or broken. The advantage of strikes, on the other hand, is in their speed. Their shortcoming lies in the comparatively lesser power they pack. The karateka must be cognizant of all these points. The first step is to clearly understand the difference in his practice between the thrust and the strike.

33

The Lone Wolf

One of my favorite ads for a martial arts school—I keep a file of the strangest, wackiest, and most illustrative—is for a place purporting to teach ken-jutsu or Japanese swordsmanship. It's a comic book-style rendering of a swordsman with a Conan-esque physique, furiously swinging a sword, eyes blazing, shoulder-length hair swinging. He's a kind of mythic Dionysus. Or Zarathustra. The *Übermensch*. The solitary samurai, standing by himself against the world. The lone wolf.

It isn't just this ad, of course, that glorifies the image of the solitary warrior. From practically every Clint Eastwood movie ever made to a Navy recruitment ad I saw just yesterday, with a SEAL team member wading alone through some exotic swamp, we see the image repeated again and again. (Note to would-be SEALs: I've been in my share of swamps, in many places. None of them are, at close range, all that exotic.) But it's particularly popular in the budo in the West. I saw a title at a local bookstore recently: *The Lone Samurai and the Martial Arts*. A martial arts movie of the seventies was *Lone Wolf McQuade*. (The protagonist had a pet wolf, just in case the title was too subtle a message.) When a cine-matic series of a popular *manga* comic in Japan was subtitled into English, the translators knew what would hook Western martial arts audiences. They ignored the original title, *Child and Expertise for Rent* and went with *Lone Wolf and Cub*.

Do you need to be a psychologist to explain the appeal of this image? I doubt it. Just think about it. Much of the appeal of the budo is for adolescent mental-ities. It promises, after all, power and respect, two kinds of capital of which the average teenager—especially the male—is generally in pretty short supply. Those same adolescent males are susceptible to believing "nobody understands me," to feeling estranged and "different," to feeling like it's them against the world, and to taking a certain romantic pleasure in indulging those attitudes. Movie adver-tisers and Navy recruitment officers and martial arts dojo are happy to indulge them as well. Movies just suck a few bucks and hours of time. The Navy, once you've signed on, isn't particularly interested in fulfilling your fantasies. You learn there—and the lesson is brought home rather dramatically in places like SEAL training—that lone wolves aren't in all that much demand and that teamwork and cooperation are what makes a Special Forces warrior. Like most teenagers, those who want to be special in the Navy or elsewhere realize it isn't achieved by behaving like a lone wolf but rather by excelling within a group, as a functioning member of the group. Unfortunately, a lot of adolescents don't grow up and a lot of them end up in dojo. And so we must deal with them. Because a lot of them haven't learned that lesson.

Okay. All you guys who want to be lone wolves, line up over here. Wait a minute. If you have a whole room full of lone wolves, aren't they, by definition, no longer that? Never mind, just listen:

You young guys out there want to be lone wolves? Your choice. But I'm betting you don't know much about wolf biology. Wolves, like people, are intensely social creatures. That's why they run in packs. They feed themselves best and mate and tend to their young most successfully when they work as a group. The individual wolf is at his best when he's a part of a larger whole. A real lone wolf gets to be that way because he can't function in the pack. Maybe he's wounded or sick. Maybe—are there any wolf psychiatrists out there?—he isn't emotionally stable enough to cut it with the rest of his kind. In any event, the lone wolf in real nature is more to be pitied than admired. He's a loser, to put it bluntly. Most lone wolves succumb to disease or predation or injuries.

We know that human individuals who are part of the "pack" tend to be healthier, whether that pack takes the form of a church or a club or a dojo. Social interaction is necessary for us to develop as people. It's important because it teaches us empathy, concern for others; it gives us a sense of purpose beyond mere survival. This may be one of the central benefits of budo training in some respects. We learn how to get along with others in circumstances that are deliberately made difficult. You have to "fight" with those closest to you. You are in an antagonistic relationship which is conversely, mutually beneficial. Yes, there are many stories of warriors in Japan who went off into the mountains for inspiration in their training. The dreams and visits by goblins and various other ways were, if we can believe the legends, just that for these warriors: *inspirations*. But the arts themselves were perfected by training with others.

Now I am certainly no one to lecture about "going along with the crowd." During my own adolescence, I don't think I did much a lot of others around me were doing. Never used illicit drugs, even though they were common at that time, never drank alcohol, never even drove fast in a car. I was very much involved in activities like the budo that very, very few people were doing at that time. And I took some pride in that. It made me feel special. Different from the masses. I was a loner in that sense. Yet within the dojo, I was very much a part of a group. I had responsibilities, commitments, and a lot of good times spent with others who shared budo with me. I chose which pack I wanted to be part of, true. And I had little to do with those packs I didn't respect or care about. But that is entirely different from wandering alone.

It's particularly ironic to see the lone wolf motif used to advertise a school for a classical martial art like kenjutsu. Those responsible for an establishment like this could probably find fewer images that would illustrate just how little they understand about a classical martial ryu. These ryu, just like the ryu for flower arranging or the tea ceremony, are fundamentally places for social interaction, designed to promote a specific cause. The martial ryu is much like a small combat unit. The effectiveness of the unit does not depend on independent action.

The image of the lone samurai wielding his katana, his muscles rippling, glossy hair tumbling, is doubtless romantic. Reality is something else. All that long hair? About two weeks into a military campaign and it would be crawling with head lice. That's why a lot of samurai kept their heads shaved. That's the nature of confronting reality. What looks good in a comic book illustration, what's appealing to the childish adolescent, is often very different from the real world. Adolescents are to be forgiven for wallowing in fantasies of the Lone Wolf variety. One mark of the adult, though, is that he has chosen wisely with which pack to run.

34

Ma (Spaces)

One recent development that has marked the "Americanization" of the martial arts in general and karate in particular, has been the introduction of "musical kata." This innovation involves practitioners performing, for the entertainment of an audience invariably, various movements of karate. Sometimes the movements are recognizable kata forms; more often they are a series of movements which have been choreographed by the performer and have only a passing resemblance to real kata. Whatever, they are performed to the rhythm and beat of background music. "Karate dancing" might be another phrase for it, and a more appropriate one. Because Occidental music is played for these performances, the budoka with a heart attuned to the more traditional and classical values of the martial Ways could be expected to disparage this sort of activity. The serious martial artist *is* almost certain to be opposed to such innovations. Not, though, because the idea of musical kata is not traditional. Just because something hasn't been done before is a poor reason to oppose it, of course. No, the budoka has no use for kata performed to the beat of music for the very simple reason that such performances have no sense of what the Japanese call *ma*.

Ma, a basic of strategy in the Japanese martial arts and Ways, seems to be one of those concepts rarely taught in any conscious manner to students anymore. It is found not only in the fighting arts of Japan but in its art, and music, and architecture; even in the relationships people have with one another. Since we have begun by talking about music, we can use that to explain what ma is.

In the Occident, anthropologists tell us, our sense of a musical beat had its birth in the earliest of our nomadic civilizations. Always on the move themselves, the wandering horsemen of northern Africa and the Middle East must have patterned their music quite naturally after the rhythmic movement of the horses that trotted beneath them. Horses move with a smooth cadence that speeds up and slows down, but which invariably can be counted with the four-beat measure that matches the four legs of the animal. Today, whether music is classical or jazz, a Hungarian *czarda* or Louisiana zydeco, if it was composed in the West, it almost surely shares the common denominator of a four-beat measure. From the ancient chants of monastery monks to modern rock, the beat has indeed gone on. It has come down through the centuries to become a tempo deeply imbedded in the musical traditions of the Western world. Sometimes it is expressed as quickly as the strings of a guitar can be strummed, sometimes as pelagic as the droning of baseball fans singing the national anthem on a hot July afternoon. But the four-beat measure is always there.

In the East, however, especially in Japan, the beat of early life was not determined by the strides of galloping horses. Rather than a nomadic existence, the Japanese from the beginnings of their social civilization adopted a predominantly agricultural lifestyle. In mountainside villages and rice fields, the tempo of daily life was set by the distinctly uneven rhythms of nature; the sudden clatter of a bamboo thicket in gusts of wind, the not-quite-steady plop of rain dripping off a thatched eave, the roar of an earth tremor followed by a seemingly endless, anticipatory pause. Within the silence of the bamboo grove before and after it has been stirred by a breeze, in the stillness following an earthquake, the moments between the dripping of raindrops, there are intervals. They are spaces in time that in Japanese are called ma.

The variable rhythms of ma have found a wide currency in Japanese life. You can hear them in virtually all Japanese music. The weirdly haunting tunes of the Japanese flute, for instance, have ma in their rambling melodies and sudden pauses that are so completely different from our idea of a beat. That is because their inspiration has not been in capturing a regular pattern, but in say, the sounds of wind soughing unevenly through bamboo or pine. In the Noh theater, instead of employing conventional music to indicate a highlight in a play as might be found in Western drama, the moment is announced by the staccato sound of wooden clappers. Other Japanese arts share this sense of nature's ma. In arranging flowers or training bonsai, for instance, it is always considered poor form to use an even number of plants. Such numbers would reflect a uniformity of spacing that is deadly to a lively and vibrant sense of ma.

It should not be surprising that irregularity in timing and a sense of movement in harmony with the sounds and beats of nature are also a part of the Japanese martial Ways. During the era of the samurai, ma was demonstrated frequently in a way just as philosophically profound as in flower arrangement or in the playing of the bamboo flute. In the fighting arts, ma is expressed in the spacing between warriors meeting in battle and in the interval between an attack and defense or an attack and its follow-up. Ma is often expressed in the martial Ways as *ma-ai*, the "distance of combative engagement." Ma-ai was of critical importance in a time when the samurai had to be constantly mindful of the distancing necessary when he faced an opponent, depending upon what weapon that opponent happened to be carrying. When two swordsmen met, theirs was a comparatively close ma because of the relatively shorter length of the Japanese sword. If the weapons were spears or halberds, though, the distance of ma increased proportionally. With the bow, the warrior's judgment of ma had to be perfect. If the distance to his target was even a little bit too long or short, his arrow would either lose its killing velocity before striking the target or be blocked before its power was fully generated in flight.

At least one famous martial artist met his end due to *nukeru ma*, an "escaped sense of distancing." He was Yamada Shinryukan, an expert with the *kusarigama*. This was a composite weapon, one of the oddest produced in feudal Japan, consisting of a sickle connected to a length of chain with a weight attached at its end. The chain of the weapon Yamada held, whirling its end in a vicious circle around him in various patterns to ensnare or strike an opponent. Anyone trying to breach the long ma Yamada established with the chain would be caught or struck. As I said, however, it was the very strategy of ma that eventually defeated Yamada, when he met a fencer, Araki Mataemon, in a duel. Araki was well aware of Yamada's exploitation of ma with the sickle and chain. To overcome it, he met Yamada at the edge of a dense copse of bamboo. As soon as their fight began, Araki retreated into the bamboo. Yamada followed, realizing too late that the wide ma of his spinning chain was going to be worse than useless in the grove. The advantage of distancing went to Araki, who killed Yamada easily.

It is in the second application of ma in the martial arts that I mentioned, the intervals between successive attacks or between a defense and a counter, that brings us back to the original question of music as a suitable background for kata. Anyone who has watched the performance of a karate kata by an outstanding Japanese or Okinawan adept has seen ma in action, for karate's kata match both the rhythms of nature and the uneven, constantly fluctuating tempos of combat. In even the most basic forms of kata, there are moments contained, deliberately so, when the performer must pause or quicken his pace, break the rhythm he has established. This break in repetitive motion is the karateka's initial experience with ma. As the complexity of the forms increase, so does the execution of ma within them.

Regrettably, East and West do not always blend, at least not without a significant loss to one or both of them. Attempts to reconcile Western music with the movements of Japanese or Okinawan kata are doomed to failure, for either the music would have to be chopped up to fit the ma of the form, or the kata themselves will lose the proper ma so vital to their meaning. The forms of karate originated in a world where our four-beat measures were unknown. And while as Occidentals we are certainly able to master these kata as well as any Asian, we must do so by accepting and learning their foreign sense of ma as well.

And so, the next time you have the opportunity to see karate kata interpreted by their most qualified and gifted exponents, try to watch not just the movements, but the rhythm of ma inherent in traditional forms. If you watch with your whole body, it is possible you will begin to see why the kata do not really benefit from musical accompaniment. They have a wonderful rhythm all their own.

35

Sen (Taking the Initiative)

Sen. If you look the word up in a Japanese dictionary, you will find it defined as "priority," or "antecedence." It is a term commonly used in the budo, where it refers to an interval of timing in which initiative is seized. In the martial arts sen means specifically that decisive moment when an action is initiated. Sen, in these disciplines, is most basically divided into two kinds. There is *go no sen* (late initiative), which is the strategy of allowing your opponent to attack, and then countering. There is also *sen no sen* (early initiative), taking advantage of a gap in his defense or his movements and attacking before he strikes. These are the choices of the budoka in a combative situation.

There is some problem in translation here. By describing sen in terms of "late" and "early" initiative the budoka may come to think go no sen is of a lesser importance than sen no sen. It sounds that way as I have described it, with the implication that if he adopts a strategy of go no sen, the budoka must simply stand by and wait for something to happen, then react. Sen no sen seems to be more aggressive, a "take-charge" attitude probably more to his liking, since instead of reacting, the budoka acts.

Actually these sorts of interpretations are rather shallow and miss the point of sen, the critical initiative. In truth, both are equal. They are like two wheels connected to a single axle, each interdependent. Go no sen, often misinterpreted as standing idly and hoping to induce an attack, is no such thing. The budoka adopting the attitude of go no sen is very active. He does not merely provide an opening for the opponent to try to attack, he maneuvers himself in a way that the opponent makes the attack the budoka in go no sen *wants* him to make. He cons the opponent into attack and exposes his weakness. It is at that later interval that the counterattack of go no sen is initiated.

For example, moving against an opponent, you lower your hands and press forward, unmistakably exposing your face. It is an irresistible opportunity for your opponent. In fact, it is more than that. In effect, by advancing openly against him, you have forced your opponent to take the initiative. If he doesn't strike, you'll be so close he will be defenseless against your own attack. So strike he does, and naturally it is launched at your most attractive target. As his punch comes closer, it appears certain you will take his fist in your face. Only at the last possible moment do you shift back, just fractionally. The power of the punch is expended less than an inch from its intended target. Your opponent is exposed temporarily, vulnerable to your counter. That is go no sen, taking action by waiting.

Sen no sen, taking the early initiative, employs a different strategy, no less gutsy. In sen no sen, your opponent's attention flickers. He readjusts his stance, begins to move forward for a kick, maybe only blinks. At that crucial instant, you strike. Without a thought of his possible counter, you drive in irretrievably, punching or kicking or seizing him for a throw, with absolute commitment, charging straight to your goal. This is the attitude of sen no sen, taking the initiative early.

In go no sen, you must coolly judge the exact angle and distance of your opponent's initial attack, evading it by a hair. In sen no sen, you must just as coolly ignore the possibility of his blow, wedging yourself past it. Different strategies, true, but both require the same sense of timing, the same courage. Both are examples of the go-for-broke mentality of the warrior arts of Japan.

The average budoka will occasionally find go no sen and sen no sen in his practice, more by accident than anything else. The good budoka will learn to employ it deliberately and effectively in the dojo. But what of sen and the exceptional budoka? The exceptional budoka will learn to take the concept of sen beyond the confines of training and put it where all the lessons of the budo belong—in his daily life.

For instance, a budoka finds himself in a completely foreign city; no friends or plans. Many of us would hole up in a hotel room, staring at incomprehensible programs on the TV, waiting to leave for a place more familiar. The budoka knows that feeling. Yet rather than give in to it, he forces himself to go out exploring. He finds a map of the area, locates an interesting museum or a unique street of shops. He tries the local food, makes an effort to talk with the people, gets to know something about this new place. He has adopted the attitude of sen no sen, and in taking such initiative, he has learned and grown from the experience.

Perhaps this same budoka is at a large social gathering, one where he recognizes someone he wants to meet. Just approaching and introducing himself would be too forward and rude in this case. So he maneuvers himself close to a mutual friend. He waits until that friend makes an introduction for him. In doing so he accomplishes what he wants by taking the late initiative: go no sen.

It would, of course, be narrow-minded to think of human activities only in martial terms. But when we consider the wider application of concepts like sen, we should understand too, that it is narrow-minded to think of them as referring only to combat. They are, after all, infinitely more valuable within the larger and more meaningful context of our daily lives.

36

Yami (Hitting the Target)

"That way over the mountain, which who stands upon
Is apt to doubt if it be indeed a road."
                                        —Robert Browning

In the ancient Chinese text on archery which in Japanese is titled *Shagakuseiso*, there are cryptic comments about the employment of a technique of the bow and arrow called *yami*. Likewise, in the densho or teaching scrolls of the Yamato ryu of battlefield archery, the school's founder Morikawa Kozan has written of the mysterious yami in his school's method of using the bow. Morikawa noted that, when it is impossible for one reason or another to use the normal *mikomi*, the process the archer uses in sighting his target, one must immediately switch to the skill of yami.

Now you must understand that the Japanese bow used in kyudo, or archery, is extremely long and, rather than having its handgrip fixed in the middle of its length as you'd see on most bows throughout the world, the grip is considerably off-center. In other words, about two-thirds of the length of the bow is above the archer's grip, one third below. This makes a Japanese bow awkward to draw without a lot of practice. Many kyudoka today find their left arm shaking when they try to pull the string to a full draw, even with months of effort. Delivering an arrow to its target is a matter of extensive training. It requires a thorough understanding of technique. That must include grounding in the method of yami.

Literally, yami is Japanese for "eclipse." It is used figuratively as well, to mean "obscurity." What yami involves technically in kyudo is this: Normally, when sighting the target the vertical angle of the bow is set in such a manner that the sightline cuts the target in half. On a round archery target, this means the archer should be able to see one half of the target when he has settled his aim. (What he sees is a half circle, which is why this method of aiming is called *hangetsu* or "half moon.") This is the typical way of aiming at a target; it works very well when that target is stationary and at a fixed distance. What about when the target is moving, though? What about when it's coming toward you, alive and menacing? At this critical moment, according to the old scrolls and teachings, the archer must resort to yami.

In the yami method of aiming, the archer lines up his bow so that it completely obscures the target (or at least its center) to his line of sight. If you extend your thumb up from your fist and aim it at a person several feet away, closing one eye at the same time, you can "eclipse" or obscure that person to your vision. This is the basis of yami. It's sighting and releasing the arrow at the moment the target is covered by your own fist and bow.

Archers once regarded yami as something of a secret technique during Japan's feudal era. The master bowman Yasu no Yoichi, a samurai retained by the Minamoto clan, is said to have used a form of yami in a famous battle against the Taira family in the 12th century. He is supposed to have used it when he took aim at a fan bearing the Taira crest that had been pinned, as a kind of challenge, on the mast of a Taira warship. Even though he was shooting from the deck of a ship that pitched in heavy seas, his arrow hit the fan.

So much for the physical technique of yami. The old scrolls, as I said, though, hint there is something beyond the physical applications of eclipsing a target. Like most written records dealing with the martial arts, these references are little more than hints meant to instruct those who already had a grasp of the teachings of the ryu. But I think that when those warriors wrote of the wider meaning of yami, they were referring to more than just eclipsing a target to hit it. I think, too, they were hinting at some realms beyond just techniques used for shooting a bow. Perhaps they wished readers to understand there is something more to yami.

Very often in life when we become fixed on a particular goal or idea, we tend to see it in our mind constantly. If we want it badly, fear it deeply, it may always be in our consciousness. The person we want to love us, the worry about incurring an injury in the dojo, a job we're desperate to have or a grade in school we really, really want to earn; any of these and ten thousand other such concerns can become preoccupations. They live with us day and night. When this happens, remembering the lessons of yami might be worthwhile. Instead of focusing on our wants or worries, we may need to eclipse them. If we quit trying to impress the object of our desire and instead are just ourselves, chances may improve that he or she may naturally be attracted to that. Forget about the injury you fear and your body may consequently relax and strengthen itself. You may begin to move in such a way that the injury you worried about may never materialize. This is a form of yami, too. It's a mental process of blotting out the targets in life and in so doing, you may find that you are striking them squarely. And while it is an ancient aspect of using a bow, yami works just as neatly for those of us today who may never have drawn one.

37

From Where I Sit

Hey, you. The one thumbing through this book, wondering if you ought to buy it, or if you've already bought it or if someone's given it to you and you're wondering if you might want to return it and get something better. Let me ask you a question.

How alert are you?

—Gichin Funakoshi would habitually walk wide around corners to prevent any kind of surprise attack, even if it meant he had to come to a complete stop first and let others pass him by.

—Chosin Chibana always carried things in his left hand only so his right was always free for use in case of any danger.

—Choki Motobu rebuilt the entrance to his house in Tokyo the same way approaches to most Japanese castles were built, causing anyone coming in to make a sharp, right-angle turn that would have made it awkward for them to use a sword.

Today, any good self-defense instruction begins with an emphasis on avoiding the need for self-defense in the first place. Students ask "What do I do if someone's hiding in the back seat of my car and grabs me from behind when I'm driving?" And competent instructors say, "Look in the back seat before you get in the car." They caution us to make sure the door has closed behind us when we enter a building, lest someone sneak in before it has shut completely. Many of us, not just martial artists, have made adjustments in our approach to daily living to cope with possible threats. This is a proactive kind of thinking. It isn't paranoia. We're not talking about tight-wired, walking time bombs who wouldn't turn their backs on their own grandmothers because you never can tell if that's Granny or a cleverly disguised ninja assassin. It's proactive in the same sense we check to make sure our shoes are tied before starting a race or stick a toe in the tub to test the water's temperature before we hop in. It's just a matter of healthy, aware living. Still, the concept of taking reasonable precautions, of being aware of the possibility of danger, is one that for the serious budoka requires constant polishing.

I remember a judo shiai, a tournament many years ago where all the male contestants had to dress in the large men's room of a high school gym. There were a lot of us; we had to jostle around a bit, getting undressed, stacking clothes, and changing into our judogi. The door opened and in came Nishimoto osho. He always reminded me of a snowman. A very muscular snowman, with a round, powerful body and a round, bald head. That head swiveled around as he came in. He caught sight of a couple of boys who were standing in front of the urinals, attending to business there. In a second, he'd slipped behind them and grabbed them by the backs of their necks. Even in normal conversation, Nishimoto tended to get your attention right away. With his fist wrapped around your neck and him roaring in your ear, it's safe to say the boys were both completely absorbed. The rest of us were equally receptive.

"Hey!" he shouted. "What if I was a bad guy instead of a kindly old priest?" Since both boys were lifted about half an inch off the ground at the time, the self-description was a tad understated. "You guys need to be more serious in your training!" Then he deposited the two back onto the ground and walked out the door.

I was reminded of the osho's lesson when I read, a while back, about a currently popular form of mugging in Great Britain. It's occurring in public restrooms and it works like this: You're sitting in a restroom stall, pants down. (Yeah, I know this isn't the usual sort of topic we cover in martial arts books that are about traditions and all that sort of stuff, but are there any readers who haven't been in this position?) Two or more muggers enter the room and one kneels down right outside your stall. He dives under the opening below the door, grabbing for both your ankles. Once he gets them, he simply gives a big jerk. You, being attached to those ankles, unless you're the size of Konishiki, very likely come off the toilet quite abruptly. At the same time, your head goes smack against the wall or the plumbing fixtures behind you. Then your spine bounces off the toilet, your butt hits the floor. None of this is going to be pleasant, the less so because it is so completely what you didn't expect to be doing. At the same time, you've got one of his accomplices who's come up from under the stall's side opening. He's holding a knife, or that classic tool of the British bad guy, the hook-bladed Stanley linoleum knife against your throat. If you're lucky, all you lose are your valuables.

So, like I said, how alert are you? All you Brazilian jujutsu experts, you JKA tough guys, you mean Wing Chun hotshots. What in your curriculum do you have to pull out against that kind of attack? I've seen my share of kata. Haven't seen one that had a move designed to counter the "under the toilet stall and grab the ankles" assault. I'm willing to bet, in fact, that none of the originators of our kata considered the possibility of a public restroom attack. They were smart enough to know that they couldn't possibly cover every threat even in their own times, never mind what dangers the future might hold. So instead of specific, individual responses, their kata are devoted to organizing the body to deal with a wide range of threats. Such training is also directed at developing awareness skills. They aren't meant to be a collection of responses. They are designed to integrate physical and mental powers.

At least one part of this kind of power is found in living without a lot of gaps in our attention and in our comportment. How many people have come by and gone around you since you've been reading this? Do you remember where you've put the car keys? Are you going to be paying more attention the next time you sit?

38

The Medium and the Message

"Hello, Doctor, thanks for taking my call. My problem is my eleven-year-old Timmy. He's been hitting the other kids at school and I'm thinking about enrolling him in a karate class to improve his self-discipline. What do you think?"

The doctor, who dispenses advice over the radio on a program I hear sometimes, thought the karate school was a wonderful idea for a "troubled ute" like Timmy. I wasn't surprised. Self-discipline is among the most popularly repeated motivations cited for getting children into karate training. That the art of the empty hand instills qualities like self-control, anger management, civility, and good citizenship seems to be accepted as obvious. Not only children, but adults as well are encouraged to practice karate for these reasons. It's even shown up as a class offered in prisons. The general public seems to accept that all that kicking and punching they see in karate schools is somehow forging better human beings in both a spiritual and emotional sense.

Well, I haven't been practicing karate that long myself. But the fact is—and I realize this borders on heresy to admit it and maybe I'm just stupid—I've never been able to understand how kicking and punching, how learning to hit others more effectively, is supposed to make better human beings. I mean, if percussive violence is a pathway to personal excellence in our species, shouldn't the current heavyweight boxing champion be a near-saint rather than the ill-mannered, arrogant lout and probable criminal that he is? (Actually, as I'm writing this, I think the title is up for grabs. I'm confident whoever has it by the time you read this will fit the description above.)

Of course, I'm being overly simplistic. The truth is that boxing gyms have turned a lot of lives around and I don't doubt some better personalities have been forged in karate dojo. I like to think that in some ways, I'm one of them. But it's overly simplistic too, to believe karate and other martial Ways are in and of themselves some sort of magical therapy. The fact is, ten years spent kicking and punching is probably going to make you a better kicker and puncher. But there is simply no logical or empirical reason to suspect it is going to mold citizens who are a social or aesthetic credit to their kind. To do so is to confuse the medium with the message.

A good example of what I'm talking about is found in the *Karate Kid* movies. In these films, you'll remember, an aimless young boy finds a whole new set of values, a more mature grasp of the concept of manhood, and a sense of respect for himself and others through his karate teacher. It's heartwarming. And it seems to prove the opposite of my point, for here is an instance of karate as a means of character building. Viewers, karateka among them, have accepted this as a fictional depiction of real-life karate training benefits. If you agree, I'd urge you to watch the movies again. You will see that the young character's real changes come through his exposure to the traditional Japanese culture of which his teacher is a representative. He finds that while his sensei is a war hero, for example, he does not brag. That while the man's wife died tragically, he doesn't complain or feel sorry for himself. The boy is exposed to the patience and discipline needed to produce bonsai or perform the tea ceremony. He is introduced to these concepts, ideas, and values the mother on that radio talk show wanted for her child, *not* because they are an inherent part of karate (although they should certainly be reflected in karate). No, his introduction to self-discipline, integrity, sensitivity to others, and all that other good stuff comes because they are integral, essential aspects of the Japanese (and Okinawan) culture that created karate and the other budo.

Developing a sense of empathy and respect for others and oneself, humility, self-control, and discipline; these are values held in esteem in Japanese culture. Of course, they are highly regarded in most cultures as well. But they are internalized and expressed in ways unique to the civilization of Japan. Those Japanese who take up an art like karate have had a perception of these values instilled in them as a natural process of acculturation. When they are taught by others who have had similar experiences, they have a good chance of passing along these values—or at least a respect and appreciation for them—to another generation of karateka when they reach the teaching level themselves. When karate is taught by these kinds of people and to people who have a cultural sensitivity to the values we're discussing, then those values *are* transmitted along with the punching and kicking and all the rest of the physical aspects of karate. Karate, under these circumstances, does provide an opportunity to produce better human beings. So do all the other forms of budo or the tea ceremony or any of the other many *Do* forms of Japan. That's one reason why some traditional martial artists also train in some of these other forms, like calligraphy or *ikebana*. No matter what the medium, the message—the inculcation and polishing of moral and social values—is the same.

However, what happens when aliens come to Japan without a sensitivity to those values? What happens when those outsiders see the medium—extraordinary feats of kicking and punching, for example—and they assume that those feats are the message and not just the medium? Or equally frustrating, what happens when Japanese teachers come to an alien culture like that of the West, with their own misconceptions? Their own mistaken notions that include a belief those aliens aren't really capable of absorbing the message of those values and who therefore concentrate their teaching only on the more shallow and superficial aspects of the medium? Sound familiar? It should. That, in some large part, is exactly what *has* happened and that is why so many American karateka and that general public about which we spoke earlier have confused the medium with the message. They go on, kicking and punching, assuming it is somehow going to teach them the values when it will not and—without an understanding of the culture behind the kicking and punching—it never will.

I do not mean to imply that traditional Japan is the only culture that has produced these values and ethics. I certainly would not suggest that Japanese karateka are always or even mostly excellent examples of these values and ethics. (Some of them are among the biggest jerks I've ever met.) Other cultures have produced similar concepts. And moral exemplars exist among those who've never trained in any kind of budo, obviously. But the approach of the budo like karate to these values is unique. The martial Ways also offer benefits to the individual willing to follow them that cannot be duplicated through any other process. Neither do I wish to insinuate only Japanese are capable of understanding traditional Japanese values or that someone must make an effort to "become Japanese" to gain access to those values. Anyone willing to open themselves to another culture can achieve this goal. But he must be sure he has apprenticed himself to a teacher who has himself become, in important ways, a product of that culture. If that teacher has acquainted himself only with the physical side of karate, no matter how skillful, he cannot possibly do anything important beyond teaching others to punch and kick. He is using the medium but sadly and all too frequently in modern karate dojo, there is only the dimmest and most inaccessible concept of the message.

39

Budo and Bach

The inability of a lot of Westerners to "get" the essence of karate and the budo has been a routine subject here. I've addressed the problems I see in transmitting one culture's arts to another society several times. So many times, in fact, readers may think I believe Westerners are a stump-dumb bunch of barbarians who could never truly appreciate the deep and profound mysteries of the budo. That's not so. I tend, in fact, to believe the unique society that is America's offers citizens a greater potential for exploring other cultures than any other. (I know, for instance, Americans who can spot a Shigaraki ceramic pot from a block away, who know every step of its creation and who have mastered the techniques. I don't know a single Japanese ceramist who has similar qualifications for, say, Appalachian folk pottery. Look at the Western authorities we have on budo. Are there corresponding experts in Japan on say, weapons and tactics of the American Revolution? I don't think so.)

No, I have no quarrel with the West. I have instead, a contention. My contention is that it is extremely difficult to understand some aspects of another culture and that misunderstandings, which are frequent, are apt to have unexpected and undesirable consequences. This is the case when Westerners try to learn deeply and thoroughly something from the East. It also happens when Easterners try to master a Western art. . . .

"There are a lot of people who practice faithfully and with desire, but I wonder if they really have a feel for it," or "It's impressive superficially, but it's actually still quite shallow" are quotes you might think I or others have written about Westerners in karate. Actually, they're from Japanese musicians, talking about Western music as it's performed in Japan.

If you've never been there and are given to stereotypes, you could believe music in Japan consists primarily of *taiko* drumming and bamboo flute tunes.

Truth is, Western classical music is enormously popular in Japan. There are ten professional symphonies in Tokyo alone. At New Year's, it's hard to walk a block anywhere without hearing a public performance of "Ode to Joy." Products from whisky to soap all use Western classical music for advertising there; every high school in Japan has a classical orchestra. The music of Beethoven, Brahms, and Bach are as well-known to Japanese as any native composer and not just among the more adult audiences classical music tends to attract here. Japanese symphony halls attract substantial numbers of young college and high school fans. It might seem Western classical music has been completely adopted and assimilated into Japanese culture. Look more closely, though, and you get a different perspective.

Several Japanese critics note that for many Japanese, especially those younger ones, concerts are more about socializing than enjoying or appreciating the music. They also complain that Japanese performers are mechanical; their music, though technically "correct," never shows any individuality. "The principal defect of Japanese performers," says one critic, "is that they never seem to have strong opinions about the music they play." Takashi Funayama, a music professor at the Tokyo University of Arts compared classical music in Japan to a blossom floating on a pond. "It's big and very beautiful," he said, "but it has no roots."

Interesting, isn't it? Many of the same criticisms others and I have made about budo imported to the West are made by Japanese critics concerning Western music imported to Japan. This isn't a coincidence, I suspect.

A lot of non-Japanese budoka are vocal in their assertion that martial arts transcend culture. They dismiss the native culture of the budo as, at best, a superfluity. They are correct: the movements and lessons and spiritual path provided by the budo are open to all who are sincere and dedicated. They are wrong, however, in asserting the attendant culture of the martial arts has no weight. The Westerner who has been raised in a civilization deeply dyed in the hues of Christianity (even though he may not be a Christian himself) has a different "feel" for music that was inspired and composed in the paradigms of that civilization. The religion that inspired the music influences it. The culture in which the music was written and in which it has been performed for centuries has also had a pervasive influence on more than just the notes and composition. A familiarity with that religion and a lifelong conversance with that culture provide insight and perspective on the music that are very, very difficult for one not similarly equipped.

Does all this mean an ensemble in Keokuk, Iowa, will intrinsically, automatically perform Bach's Minuet in G Major better, more authoritatively than one in Kyoto? Nope. It means that the folks in Keokuk will have a perception and a shared understanding of aspects of the music that are difficult for a non-Westerner to grasp. Not impossible to grasp. But more difficult. It is profoundly ignorant to believe one's race or place of birth somehow convey a special, privileged power for mastering or understanding aspects of culture. Conversely, it is profoundly arrogant to believe each of us is automatically equal in approaching the world's very different, unique cultures.

This is a challenge we face in trying to master budo like karate-do. The obstacles we encounter in overcoming our unfamiliarity with Japanese culture are not insurmountable. We are not doomed, by virtue of our birthplace, never to "get" the real stuff, never to penetrate the depths. We must acknowledge, though, that the budo has had a fostering culture very different from our own. We must realize that the influences that culture has had on budo have not been incidental. And we must understand that we don't come to the dojo with a complete set of cultural decoders that enable us to break down the barriers that stand in our way.

It's a daunting task. More formidable, arguably, than the one faced by Japanese musicians trying to get at the heart of Bach's music. Are you up to it?

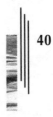

40

The Kata as a Training Tool

The serious karateka is always searching for methods to improve his training. Typically, many modern practitioners look around for new ways, for the latest in up-to-date technologies. It is one of the most lamentable illnesses of our time that people in this century can see their world only in a linear progression. The past is something to be forgotten or improved upon; only the future provides lessons of worth for them.

Those who follow a timeless path like the budo know better. Very often the most valuable lessons can come from going into the past, taking a cyclical view of things. While the karateka may recognize the value of his kata in some regards, for instance, he may not realize that among its other attributes it can also be an excellent tool for his aerobic training.

The usual approach to practicing kata is to go through it with proper speed, focus, and power, one or more times. Sometimes the kata is repeated again and again (particularly if the karateka's repertoire at that stage of his training is limited). Other practice sessions may call for performing all of the kata known to the practitioner, one after another. There is nothing wrong with either of these approaches: they are probably the only ways to learn a kata's "outer movements" and to memorize the individual kata's place in the curriculum of the karate style. Once well-learned, however, the kata's worth as a training device emerges.

Go through the movements of the kata as you normally would, for instance. Pick a simple one to begin with, using 20–30 separate motions. Perform at the regular speed or a little slower if you like. Only this time in your practice, use only enough energy to do the action. No snap, no power, no focus at all. Sounds like your kind of training, you say. There is a catch, however. Once you are finished, repeat the kata; then again. Repeat it say, about 25 times. That may not sound too tough, either. This method of practice will probably not sound that challenging through the first five or six repetitions. After all, you are just moving without any force at all. But somewhere in there, along about the ninth or tenth repetition, your breath will start to get a little labored. You will start to think that that kata has more moves than it seemed. Don't stop. As soon as one kata finishes, begin it again. When you finish—if you finish—you will have a deeper understanding of the form. And you will see too, how the kata can be an excellent means of building stamina.

Another way of training with the kata depends upon your grasp of all its parts. Once you have learned them thoroughly (and again, the most basic kata will suffice for beginning this), approach the kata from a different way. Let's use as a good example the very basic kata taught in nearly all Japanese and Okinawan karate dojo, the Heian or Pinan *shodan* kata. First move: turn to the left; downward block. Step forward; lunge punch. Now, instead of continuing, go right back to the start of the form. Do the same three moves, ten times in a row. Then repeat them again and go onto the next three moves of the kata. Then repeat that sequence, ten times, too, pulling it out of the kata, and so on. As you concentrate on these little sections of the kata, you will begin to see things about it that may, in ordinary practice, be overlooked. What moves first when the kata begins? Are you turning your head in the direction of the block before executing it as you should? Does the knee turn into the block, driving the hips toward it?

This kind of kata training, isolating two or three individual movements from the entire form and subjecting them to a concentrated repetition, quickly becomes exhausting. Yet the physical challenge practicing in this variation is different from the weariness brought on by repeating the entire kata without force. Both these methods, though, serve to illustrate how the kata can be manipulated as a tool in your training. They cannot replace your regular kata practice, and are not meant to. Use them, though, to round out your training—and to expand you appreciation of what a valuable facet of karate they truly are.

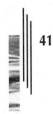

41

The Original Okinawan Karate Dojo

My two Okinawan karate teachers often liked to make the point that karate is, to be exact, not Japanese but Okinawan in origin. As my training with them went on, they also began to explain to me that there are many words in the Okinawan language for which there are no adequate equivalents in other tongues, not even in Japanese. This has led to some gaps in the knowledge of karateka. So it is worthwhile to take a look at the language the first karateka spoke and used.

First, understand there is no single Okinawan language; neither should we speak of the region correctly as "Okinawa." Karate's birthplace is actually the Ryukyus, a number of small islands off the coast of southern Japan. There are nearly a dozen dialects recognized here, some spoken only on islands not much larger than the borough of Manhattan. Okinawa is the largest island of the Ryukyuan archipelago, the cultural and social center of the chain. Second, all Okinawan languages, phonologically speaking, are dialects of ancient Japanese. But the Okinawans adapted Japanese, so much so that when Okinawan is spoken today it is virtually unintelligible to a Japanese speaker. It is not, however, spoken all that often, for not only is Okinawan a unique set of dialects, it is also a language in danger of extinction. Most Okinawans born after the Second World War speak standard Japanese with just a few Okinawan words or idioms thrown into their daily speech. To hear much Okinawan you must go to the more traditional places in the Ryukyus: potteries or looms where native craftsmen turn out unique arts. Okinawan karate dojo are a source for original culture too, but caution must be exercised in determining what fighting arts terms are authentically Okinawan and which are Japanese imports or adaptations.

The word *dojo*, for instance, is a Japanese word and concept. (Its origins are Buddhist, incidentally. The main worship hall of a Buddhist temple is referred to as a dojo, and it is written with the same characters meaning, "a place to follow the Way.") Where did Okinawans in the old days practice their karate? Often they did it at a *miya*. To understand what a miya is all about, you must know something about Ryukyuan life and religion. Houses on these islands have traditionally been set low to the ground in comparison with homes on mainland Japan. They are also surrounded usually by thick walls of plaster or sometimes coral block, all to protect against annual typhoon which tend to rake across the Ryukyus with a particular viciousness. Karate training was sometimes conducted in the courtyards behind these walls, safe and secret from prying eyes. But the center of every Okinawan village was its *umui*. This was doubtless a corruption of the Japanese word *omori,* meaning a grove or a thicket. But an umui was a special place, the dwelling of deities. Umui were actually natural temples, places of worship. Umui were always located on a hilltop and by religious custom on Okinawa, that hill had to have *kuba*, a short, runty kind of palm, and *mani*, or boxtree growing on it. The umui was sacred, the spiritual focus of the village where its protective gods were believed to reside.

Within the umui was a clearing where religious activities were held. This clearing was the miya, where local karate training was also conducted. (The Miyagi family is well-known in both karate history and in fiction, as in Chojun Miyagi and the "Miyagi sensei" familiar to filmgoers. Well, Miyagi is a Japanese version of the original Okinawan name, Miyagusuku. It means "the protector of the miya.")

Think of how well the custom of conducting karate training in the precincts of the umui worked for the Okinawans. The umui was, by its fundamental nature, secluded and sacred. Only a local inhabitant would go there. The miya, inside the umui, was even more private. Training, usually done at night after work, by lantern light, was safe from any spying by possible enemies who were almost certain to be coming from outside the village. Further, practice was done in front of the village deities who would keep you on your toes and look affectionately upon your efforts.

It was very far from Okinawa where I began my own practice of karate. Even so, my sensei liked to practice with me in a cemetery near their home. If there were spirits around us, among them was a fellow shot by Wild Bill Hickok who was buried there. But it was a miya of sorts, I suppose. And I felt closer to all the Ryukyuan karateka of old for practicing and learning in such a place.

42

Some Advice

Your sensei does not know everything.

Sorry to be so blunt about this. But it is really a concept you ought to consider. I'm not saying your teacher isn't qualified to instruct you in your karate training. I'm sure he or she is quite skilled in that regard. I'm not talking about your sensei's abilities in punching or kicking or body movement or in teaching any of those. No, I am referring to his ability to give advice on matters like your love life, your choice of a career, your efforts to stop smoking.

Of course, your particular sensei might be able to offer some very good advice on these or on other personal matters in your life. You know and trust him, I assume. So it's reasonable you would seek him out if you need some counseling or just want someone to listen. In this sense, a karate teacher is much like anyone else with whom you might want to talk. But keep this in mind: your karate teacher has not gone to "sensei school" where he took classes in how to help people with their personal problems or decisions. He is probably very wise in the art of karate. But his insights into who you ought to marry or to which school you ought to apply to next fall; his wisdom about men or women, these are in all probability not much different from the advice you might get from your parents, from a minister or a rabbi, or from a mental health care worker or a therapist. Remember too—and this is crucial—that in most cases while these latter individuals will give you their opinions, they do not presume to give you advice when you have not asked for it. (Okay, well maybe your parents have been known to give you some pointers on this or that when you have not actually sought them out, but you know what I mean.)

I mention all this because for some reason, a lot of martial arts teachers come to believe they have some special abilities beyond their teaching of the art. They behave as though they have almost a right and certainly a duty to counsel and advise and even dictate to their students in all sorts of personal areas of those students' lives. They become like some sort of weird combination of Wise Old Shaman and Daddy Figure. Benevolent Village Elder and Stern Authority. I have heard of sensei telling students when and whom to marry, that they should seek a divorce, that they should put off their schooling or find a different job. I'm astounded that students would actually respond to this behavior, as if the sensei had some legal or moral authority over them. But I suppose it's under-standable in some respects.

I suspect there are two reasons why sensei begin to behave in this fashion. The first has to do with the way in which we have long approached sports in the West. Beginning with the Greeks, we have considered sports as both an analogy and a training ground for real life. Sports teach us to be a gracious winner and a stoic loser; they teach teamwork and virtue and all that. So it's hardly remark-able that we would regard the authority figure in sports—the coach—as a kind of Aristotelian mentor and father figure. It is not a stretch at all for the sensei to be perceived as a "coach." That, in fact, is how most martial artists, if they were asked to explain the place of the sensei in the dojo, would do it. He is a coach. The connection is obvious, as are its ramifications. Sensei represents not just one who teaches us the technical aspects of his art. He is the one who guides us into a deeper understanding of life. When you treat a person this way, it isn't sur-prising that he responds by acting the part. Put a sensei in the same category you do a coach (who, not incidentally, is most often interacting with athletes younger and less experienced in life than he is) and the sensei will take on the responsibilities you appear to be asking of him.

Secondly, there is all the folderol of "Oriental" mysticism that surrounds the sensei. He is Mr. Miyagi and Yoda and whoever that blind guy was who was David Carradine's professor at Shaolin University on *Kung Fu*. He is all-knowing. He has the answers. If he can teach you, give you the self-confidence to put your fist through a stack of boards, is it too much to accept that he knows as well whether you and your spouse should have kids now or wait a few years?

It is not merely the students' beliefs about their teacher that builds this aura of the sensei as an omnipotent Ann Landers. The sensei can too, if he is less than scrupulous, promote it. (In fact, let's be honest: even if you *are* a person of scru-ples and virtue, it's awfully easy to fall into the trap unconsciously set by adoring students.) It's hugely enjoyable to tell other people what to do, how to run their lives. It's not just a lot of fun, it's also a way of reinforcing your own status and sense of self. The sensei's image among his students is enhanced and fortified by his role as an advice-giver. Being consulted on personal matters also gives the sensei more power, more control over those under him. The sensei who is indispensable in making decisions about areas of your life outside training gains a control over you that extends beyond, far beyond the hours you actually spend under the sensei's tutelage in the dojo.

Unfortunately, this is rarely a healthy development for you, for the sensei, or for the entire dojo. The karateka is supposed to be expanding his own sense of self, his power of control over his life. This is true of any budoka. It is the sensei's job to guide this growth. When the sensei exerts his own control over the student, though, he is working in precisely the opposite direction.

It is critical to avoid falling (or being led) into the trap of allowing Sensei to make decisions for you that you ought to be making for yourself. You must recognize the signs. You must acknowledge the very natural human tendency to let others make hard choices for you instead of confronting those choices yourself. From your sensei you must expect and demand to be treated as a student—not as a child or as a ward. If you cannot take responsibility for your own life, you have no business trying to follow the Way of karate. If your teacher cannot allow you that responsibility, he has no business trying to lead you there.

43

Telegraphing

The class was devoted to the subject of some joint locks and pins that are concealed within the kata *Empi*. One was a neat little trick that had the attacker ending up flat on his face; one arm pinned in a particularly uncomfortable fashion, very much like the *osae-waza*, or pinning techniques, common in aikido. The attacker's arm was captured in such a way that it was pulled up and away from his body. The karateka performing this technique had only to stretch and rotate the captured arm a little bit and the pain was instantly intense. It was almost as if an electric shock had passed through the whole body. That's what must have been happening to one of the guys because just before he would tap on the floor to signal his submission, his body would spasm, both legs jerking up at the knees.

"Don't do that!" the sensei snapped. Despite his pain, the karateka managed to laugh. "What do you mean?" he asked. "It was an involuntary response."

"Maybe," the sensei said. "But you're telegraphing."

Anyone who has spent much time in almost any combative art is familiar with this term: telegraphing. In the Japanese budo it is sometimes referred to as *mibune*, which means, "to make a sign or gesture." It means to give away your intentions unconsciously to your opponent, sending a signal out that he can pick up and interpret the way a telegraph sends out a coded message. (The term is hopelessly outdated, isn't it? How many of you have ever sent or received a telegram? Maybe within a few more years we will be calling this phenomenon "faxing.")

A karateka will dip his shoulder just before he's going to punch. A kendoka will tap his weapon's tip against that of his opponent's just prior to launching a strike: these are obvious examples of telegraphing. But sometimes the signals are subtler. One karateka I knew could always be depended upon to tug at the top of his trouser thigh just before he was going to kick with that leg. Another judoka I faced in tournaments would invariably blink his eyes before he tried any foot sweeps. No other attacks, just the foot sweep. You could count on it every time and many of us who fought him did just that, beginning our counter as soon as we saw the blink.

Obviously, telegraphing imposes a real handicap on the martial artist, especially since these messages are nearly always unconscious actions. We're not aware that we're sending them. If your opponent knows ahead of time (even if it's only a fraction of a second) that a technique is imminent, he has a tremendous advantage over you. (This is a reason, incidentally, why more traditional karateka do not develop that rhythmic "bouncing" of boxing, hopping up and down as can be seen at many karate tournaments. The hopping motion creates a rhythm, one that must be broken before any attack begins. The opponent catches the rhythm and knows instantly when it is disrupted. Bouncing is fine for boxers and others trying to score points. But it is a strategy fraught with danger when applied to a real conflict, in part because telegraphing is its natural and undesirable by-product.)

As is clear from the examples I just gave, we're accustomed to thinking of telegraphing as a precipatory signal. The dipping shoulder, the blink; they give advance warning of an action about to happen. Why then, was the karateka told he was telegraphing even after the technique was completed and when it was performed against him? The reason is that the budoka does not want to give away *any* clues, no matter what his situation, to his opponent. Let us say, for instance, that in a fight your attacker has succeeded in locking your arm and, in your efforts at escaping, he's managed to break the limb. In a bar brawl or a sidewalk fight of the sort macho young men with too much time and testosterone on their hands are apt to be involved, a broken arm would be a matter of grave concern. Yet we must remember that in a serious, life-and-death encounter, a broken arm is among the least of the injuries you must expect.

Not only must the martial artist accept the probability of a serious injury, he must be psychologically prepared to conceal its effects from his opponent. "You cannot always keep an enemy from wounding you," goes an adage from one classical school of swordsmanship, "but you can keep him from *knowing* he's wounded you." This is important; think about it. You employ a strike against an attacker that connects and breaks a bone. You're sure of it, you felt the break when you hit, heard the snap. Now, this happens against an opponent who screams and clutches the injured limb, then he steadies himself to continue the fight. Or, you break the limb the same way against an attacker who, even as you strike, does not flinch. He shows no emotion at all, he simply continues the fight. From an emotional, psychological point of view, which enemy would you rather face? Obviously, the attacker who has absorbed the injury (or who at least is not allowing its effects to show) is a formidable foe. Maybe he's dying inside or maybe he really *has* felt no pain. You've no way of knowing and you're going to think twice before continuing the encounter.

There will be those who note that dojo training is not the same as a real fight. Nor should it be. Nor does ignoring pain make you anything but staggeringly stupid. To continue training stoically with a broken arm is the stuff of which macho guys like to recount in bull sessions. The reality is that further traumatizing that kind of injury or failing to have it treated properly is to risk permanent, chronic problems. But that, you see, is one of the most outstanding features of budo like aikido and judo, and it is one reason why studying the grappling and joint locks found in karate's kata are a vital aspect of training in that art. Just as one partner learns to inflict pain by degrees, in a controlled manner, the receiver learns to absorb it with the same, gradually increasing control. (This is why too, no martial artist can consider his training complete, no matter how expansive, unless it includes one of the grappling arts.)

There is a method for letting your training partner know the level of pain he's inflicted is sufficient to subdue you and that more will cause injury. You tap the mat or an available part of his or your own anatomy. It is a voluntary, conscious action, unlike the sudden intake of breath, the surprised cry, the spastic jerking of an undisciplined body. Tapping is a kind of telegraphing, true, but it is deliberate. Any other expression of pain received is counterproductive to training. It gives your dojo partner a message he should be getting instead through your tapping. It can give a real opponent in a real fight the kind of information you never want him to have.

44

A Few Stories . . .

When we read or are told tales of the great martial artists of the past, we may get a rather narrow view of their personalities. It is one thing to learn of the wonderful accomplishments of a person; another entirely to know what kind of *person* he was. The judo legend Mifune Kyuzo, for instance, sometimes used to sleep on a wooden beam that braced the ceiling in his home, testing his balance even in slumber. If he overrelaxed while he slept, he would wake up with a painful fall. The sword master Yamaoka Tesshu was going about his daily training as he had for most of his life, even in the final weeks when cancer was eating away at his stomach. These seem to be *serious* guys. True enough, they were. But they were, as are most remarkable and successful people, outstanding in their sense of humor too. It is regrettable, especially as the times in which they lived grow further and further distant from us, separating us even more from their memories, that the more lighthearted and humorous aspects of their lives are so little known. Knowing this more "human" side of masters of the past gives us a more balanced portrait of them. It can also be instructional, for very often their pranks and clowning have a message for us.

Jigoro Kano, the founder of modern judo, was a man of very good taste and refinement. We have photos of him wearing both traditional Japanese clothes and Western suits, and in each, he looks perfectly at home. He was well-educated and knowledgeable about the ways of the world beyond Japan. Witty and urbane, he had little use for the violent and coarse thugs who advertised themselves as "jujutsu masters" and who went about to various dojo in Meiji Japan, offering challenges or thinly disguised threats and intimidation. He was also skeptical of the contests of strength that many of these martial artists used to try to prove their skills. One such fellow visited Kano and boasted that he could shatter a foot-high stack of roofing tiles. Was Kano interested?

Tiles used on the roofs of Japanese houses are made of hard-baked ceramic. They are curved and about a couple of inches thick. Breaking stacks of them has long been a display of strength similar to the board-breaking more familiar to many of us in the West. Kano said he would indeed like to see such a feat. After some of his students assembled a stack of tiles the requisite height, the visitor made a show of warming up, taking several practice strokes at the stack and then finally, with a dramatic flourish, smashing through them with his fist. He turned to Kano triumphantly, expecting that he would soon have most of Kano's students practicing under his instruction. "Can you do that?" he sneered.

"I believe I can," Kano said. He instructed his students to assemble another stack of the tiles, first excusing himself, he said, to "loosen up" in private. When he returned Kano poised himself above the tiles, staring intently at them. He paused, and then with a lightning move he reached into his kimono, pulled out a hammer he'd hidden there, and used it to break the tiles.

"That wasn't your fist!" the visitor accused.

"Of course not," Kano replied. "Only an idiot would risk damaging his bare hand when there is a tool available for the job."

Roofing tiles played a role in an episode in the life of Kyuzo Mifune, Kano's most brilliant disciple and the last judoka to be awarded the 10th dan, the highest grade ever awarded in judo. Mifune had responded to the request of a jujutsu dojo to come and demonstrate the new judo that Kano was still, at that time, in the process of creating. After he had displayed the throws and grappling techniques of judo, Mifune answered questions from the jujutsu exponents. One of them noted that their style of martial art stressed strikes, and methods used to strengthen the body against blows. He wanted to know if Mifune could absorb a punch to the stomach. The jujutsu adept offered to demonstrate his ability to do the same first. Mifune agreed. The man was powerfully built and had a row of rigid abdominal muscles that were visible even under his training jacket. He looked like he could take the blow of a big temple bell striker without much damage. Another volunteer cocked his fist and drove it hard into the adept's midsection. The blow resounded with a dull *thump* through the dojo. It did not seem to faze the jujutsu man in the slightest.

"Let me borrow your toilet a moment," Mifune said, and after he'd excused himself, the jujutsu dojo erupted into laughter. They knew the man who'd challenged Mifune was particularly skillful at punching; the slight, skinny

Mifune would not stand a chance. Upon Mifune's return, however, they sat quietly, their sober faces hiding the pleasure they were looking forward to.

"Go ahead," Mifune said, settling himself into the front-facing judo stance of *jigotai*, his knees slightly bent, back straight. "I'm ready."

The punch was, as the entire dojo expected, a mighty one. It came whistling in and everyone present expected the slender Mifune to be hurtled through a wall. But when the fist met Mifune's stomach, there was only a dull *clunk*! Mifune did not fly back. He did not even blink. The group gathered in the dojo was astounded. The jujutsu exponent who had hit Mifune was incredulous. Mifune's midsection, he thought, had felt like a brick . . . or a tile, to be more exact. With a big smile, Mifune reached into the folds of his kimono and pulled out a roofing tile he had found and hidden there on his trip to the toilet.

The Okinawan karateman Sokon Matsumura once played a prank on the ruler of the Ryukyus. The king owned a huge bull of which he was immensely proud. Bulls were a status symbol on Okinawa at that time. They were raised and pampered like members of the family and they were used for sport and fought in contests. On Okinawa, bullfighting consisted of pitting two bulls against each other, a spectacle that is still seen on the island. It is not quite so bloody as it sounds. The bulls are led into a dirt ring and placed almost nose to nose. The "fight" is sometimes that; more often the bulls push against one another until one either gives way or is driven to its knees. Death or injury of either animal is rare. The king, however, mindful of Matsumura's legendary karate prowess, suggested a variation. He challenged Matsumura to fight his bull. After thinking if over, Matsumura consented to the match, to be held several days later. A few days after he accepted the challenge, Matsumura slipped quietly into the stables of the king. He bribed a stable keeper into allowing him into the paddock with his future and four-footed opponent. Approaching the animal carefully, the karate master produced a sharp pin with which he jabbed the bull on its soft nose. The bull, surprised, bellowed in pain, and Matsumura retreated. But he returned again the next day, repeating the same jab, a treatment he continued until the day of the match.

A huge crowd had assembled for the fight between man and beast. As a group, they turned to watch the king's bull come pacing out of its pen, snorting and pawing. Surely, they all thought, this fierce demon of a bull will stomp Matsumura into the dirt. When Matsumura entered the arena, though, the bull caught his scent. Remembering the pain associated with the smell of this man, the animal promptly lowered his head and scrambled for the oppo-site side of the arena, racing frantically to get away from Matsumura.

"It was incredible," the spectators would later recall. "That animal sensed Matsumura's power as soon as he appeared. That bull fled in terror!" And the karate master's reputation continued to grow.

Never one to pass up an opportunity to play a joke was Yamaoka Tesshu, the founder of the Itto Shoden Muto ryu of swordsmanship. Tesshu was a large man for his time, nearly six feet tall. He also sported a long, full beard, and in daily wear, he often favored Western clothes instead of a kimono and hakama. And so one evening when Tesshu dropped by to watch a neighborhood sumo contest, he appeared very much to be one of the foreigners who were beginning to come to Japan in the late 19th century.

The matches Tesshu watched that night were dominated by one wrestler, a local champion who had bested every opponent he had faced. Full of himself, the wrestler stood at the side of the ring and addressed the crowd. "Any chal-lengers in the crowd this evening?" he asked, which brought a roar from the spectators. The noise abruptly stopped when Tesshu responded by leaping into the ring; then returned, louder than before.

"A foreigner!" they shouted, delighted at the prospect of a Western barbar-ian being defeated by one of their own sumo champs. But the crowd, of course, was in for a surprise on that particular evening. Yamaoka Tesshu was a master swordsman. Years of training had brought his body to a fine edge. He had phe-nomenal control of his balance and often challenged his own students to try to upset his posture. After practice, two or three of them would make a game of pushing and pulling at Tesshu from different directions, failing to move him. And so it was that every sumo wrestler in the contest that night went home, faces red with shame, all of them wondering at their inability even to budge that mysterious and powerful foreigner. . . .

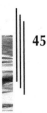

45

Earning a Black Belt

It's midsummer as I write this, time for lolling at the swimming hole, fresh tomatoes, and cattle mutilations. At least here in the Midwest, summer's a slow news period. So every July, it seems, we get "news" stories about mysterious cow deaths on farms around here, peppered with quotes from UFO authorities who hint there may be extraterrestrial vandalism behind it all. If your papers carry similar stories, you know summer is also when you can depend on headlines like "A Black Belt—And He's Only Eight Years Old!" There will be a cute little local interest story about the just-promoted youngster, probably with a photo of him kicking through a stack of boards.

Critics will insist no child could possibly have the emotional maturity to attain a black belt rank. They'll observe too, with some cynicism, that such articles inevitably mention the child's school and instructor. It's a convenient bit of free advertising as canny martial arts teachers know when they call the paper to alert them to the "story." Supporters, however, will maintain that if the instructor feels the child's qualified, that should be all that's necessary. They'll note such articles can serve to draw other young people to the art, and so on.

These arguments pro and con, seem to me to be missing a point relevant to anyone who teaches or operates a martial arts school. That point is: How hard would you be willing to work for something that's attainable by a child? If an instructor really feels that a youngster not yet into puberty is worthy of a black belt ranking in an art, what does that say about the sophistication and profundity of the art? What would you think of a college that awarded degrees to kids just learning their multiplication tables? I suppose the reply would be that if that kid already knew his tables, already knew in fact, all that was necessary or required to earn a degree from that college, then he ought to get the paper. I'd agree. I just wouldn't think too highly of the standards or curriculum of that college.

Before the summer is out here, I'd be willing to bet the local papers will also sport another headline, something like "Seventy-Year-Old Granny Earns Black Belt." To be consistent, we ought to ask ourselves the same question: How much is a black belt worth if it can be attained by a person of that age? This time, however, the answer is not so simple. The answer really depends upon what we mean by "earning" a black belt.

The whole mystique of the black belt has become much more an image of power and attainment in the West than in Japan. Not that ranking isn't important in Japan: it is—extremely so. But when the subject arises, an exponent of say, Goju ryu karate from Kanagawa is likely to tell you not that he's a "black belt" but that he's sandan (third level) or godan (fifth level). Within the martial arts community in Japan, the awarding of the first level (shodan) of black belt is recognition that you have a familiarity with the fundamentals of the art. (I'm speaking generally here.) When you get a black belt ranking it doesn't mean you've gotten a foot in the door. It means you have learned how to find the door-knob. Pretty much the same definition of a shodan obtains among traditionally minded martial artists in this country. Nobody who knows anything about judo or aikido or karate is going to be dazzled when you tell them you've reached shodan level. In fact, the only people who were ever impressed by a black belt were the almost absurdly uninformed general public.

This being the case, can a 70-year-old legitimately earn a black belt? If she (and we're using an older woman as an example just for emphasis) began her training in her twenties and has continued on and for some reason or another has never tested or been ranked, the answer is "of course." In all those years she has absorbed the essence of the art, if she's been training correctly, and certainly deserves the rank in almost anyone's opinion. We're obviously speaking of those who didn't come into a dojo until they were already well advanced in age. Let's say she began her karate training when she was sixty-one. And now she's before you, the grading official, testing for shodan rank. What do you do?

You must consider two convergent factors, I think. The first is her progress in maximizing her abilities. Physically, she may be able to generate 1x of power in her punch, let's say. The college student testing beside her is capable of generating 10x power in her punch. That's a big difference. But if she's actually delivering everything she's got, using good body mechanics, that granny's 1x deserves recognition. In other words, that she's got only 10 percent of the punching power of a younger karateka is not as important as is the fact she is (or isn't) delivering 100 percent of her 10 percent.

The second, equally important and contrasting factor is how close our black belt candidate comes to meeting a more objective standard for the rank. Someone whose front kick can be executed head high comes closer to that standard than one who can kick only to his own midsection level. The candidate who cannot kick above his own shin is very far from the standard, the minimum that everyone should meet. (Whether the height of one's kicks *ought* to be a standard of the art is another question entirely, isn't it?)

So the grading instructor must scrutinize both the subjective—how is this student doing what she can with what she, as an individual, has got?—and the objective—how does this student compare with the ideal? It is not an easy task. It illuminates the idiocy of the popular custom of a visiting "master" dropping in to conduct testing *en masse*. He's testing people he may never have seen before; doesn't even know their names. You think a rank's worth something from that guy, you're welcome to it. The integrity of the rank, the person wearing it, and the art it represents, all these depend in considerable degree on the ability of the instructor to evaluate his students using these criteria.

Of course, there is a third factor that must be weighed in awarding a black belt. In this aspect, the grading instructor ought to be completely selfish. He ought to be thinking of his dojo and his art. Specifically, he ought to be thinking: how will this person represent my teaching, my school, my art? I don't mean "will this person be a tough behind-kicker or a tournament champ?" (Although if that's the goal of the instructor's school, there's no surer way to get there than by promoting a bunch of thugs to black belt rank.) I don't mean "will this person be a good walking advertisement?" (Although if that's the goal, promoting to black belt a cute little kid or a blue-coiffed granny are sure attention-getters.) What I mean is: will this person, as a black belt, display the maturity and dignity that are supposed to be the hallmarks of a practitioner of this art? Of all the questions surrounding the awarding of a black belt, it seems to me this is the first one that should be asked and it must as well be the easiest to answer.

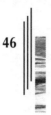

46

A Feudal Democracy:
The Dilemma of Budo
Organizations in the West

"Welcome to the first meeting of the organization I am confident will bring our Really Traditional Karate Association into the future in this country," began the chief instructor of the RTKA (US branch).

"Now I know many of you have hesitations about this," the chief went on. "You may believe you, my senior students, are still like children and I am you 'father.'"

Jim, one of the RTKA teachers in the group, nodded. As one of the chief instructor's senior students, that was exactly how he felt. Even though he operated three dojo along with a karate class at the local university, he believed he still had a lot to learn, not only in karate, but also in the business of making the RTKA a viable organization.

"But you are no longer children," the chief went on. "You have matured as karateka. Now you are ready to assume responsibilities for running this 'family' of our karate." The chief paused. "After all, I'm getting too damned old and frail!"

Everyone laughed and the chief continued. "No, this is America. We need to organize the RTKA as a democracy. I'm appointing you seniors as regional directors. You will oversee the dojo in your region and make the bylaws for the RTKA itself. I believe you are ready for this and I'm confident you will carry on the traditions of our art."

Jim was appointed regional director; in spite of his concerns about the job, he took it seriously. His sensei believed in him. He wouldn't let Sensei down. In addition to his teaching duties, he began thinking of ways the RTKA could be improved. He reasoned, for instance, that a sharing of responsibilities could streamline the organization. In the RTKA all rank promotions had to be administered directly by the chief instructor.

"All us regional directors are at least fourth dan," Jim said to one of the other directors. "Why don't we administer the promotions up to brown belt in our own regions?"

"Great idea," his colleague said. "For some of the smaller clubs in my region, it's just too expensive to bring Sensei in on a regular basis. So your plan would be good for the RTKA from an economic standpoint, too."

Together, Jim and his friend presented their idea at the next meeting of the RTKA, where it was met with considerable enthusiasm by everyone—except the chief instructor, their sensei. He said nothing. Jim brought the plan up for a vote, according to the bylaws of the RTKA. It passed, unanimously. The directors waited for the chief instructor to congratulate them on a job well done.

"No," said the sensei.

"What?" Jim asked, thinking he'd misunderstood.

"No," the sensei repeated. "I was appointed to my position by the Founder. I will run this organization as I think he would have wanted it run. There can be no changes made in the procedures for promotions."

"But Sensei," Jim said, "wasn't this organization supposed to be a democracy? Wasn't that what you said?"

"Yes," snapped the chief instructor. "But you are behaving like a naughty child. Are you forgetting that I was training with the Founder long before you were even born?"

"But Sensei," Jim tried again.

"Right. You call me 'sensei.' It is not the Japanese way to challenge one's teacher. The matter is closed. We will move on to the next item on the agenda."

Not surprisingly, Jim resigned his position as director, humiliated and disgusted. Not long thereafter, he dropped out of the RTKA altogether. On the evening following his resignation, the phone rang at the home of Roger, another RTKA teacher, less senior than Jim, who had a dojo in the same region. It was the chief instructor calling, asking Roger if he would accept a position as regional director of the RTKA. Roger protested: he wasn't qualified for such an important post.

"Of course you are," the sensei said. "You are ready to assume some responsibilities for running this 'family' of RTKA karate. After all," the sensei said, "I cannot make all the decisions. . . ."

This little drama is not exactly fact. But there are plenty of readers who will quickly tell you that it is a very long way from fiction as well. It is, in one way or another, a typical scenario of the evolution of martial arts organizations that have sprung up outside Japan. They are—let's face it—largely a collection of disasters.

The reasons for these disasters are diverse. The senior Japanese-born budo leaders in this country were raised in a monarchy. Democracy and its traditions are not even a full generation old in Japan. Then too, the budo have no real precedents to look for in establishing their organizations. Remember, the oldest budo groups in Japan are little more than 100 years old. They are still establishing themselves there in some ways. The problems of germinating offspring organizations in the West add whole new dimensions of difficulty.

What precedents the budo groups do have are to be found almost solely in the classical koryu. In koryu, the headmaster's word was and is law. He alone is responsible for all decisions in all facets of the ryu. This is typical of all feudal Japanese institutions; flower arranging, tea ceremony, and so on. The modern budo leader is tempted to look at these institutions as his model for an organization. That's what our fictional RTKA master did. However, what he overlooks is this: the goals and methods, the very essence of the koryu is distinct from that of the modern budo. No koryu founder started his school based upon the aspiration it would be of philosophical benefit to people all over the world. He had no concern for competition or ranks or for adapting his art to legions of individuals outside the caste of the feudal warrior. The budo leader, though, must contend with all these. They are the basis of his Way.

I am not a member of any budo organization. Nor am I likely to be asked to join. But if I were asked, I would ask a couple of questions in return. Let's say the RTKA chief's call came to me to get me to serve as a regional director.

"Sensei," I would say, "if I become a director, I might propose to my fellow board members that we delete kata from the RTKA. Or we might decide you *are* too old to make *any* decisions. We might vote to retire you as chief instructor. If we do any of that, what would you do?"

If the chief instructor would agree to abide by these obviously inane—but democratically board approved—decisions, I'd figure he was sincere about having a democratic budo organization. I'd still want the agreement in writing, but I'd consider serving. But if he vacillated at all, I'd pass. Because a democracy means people making wrong decisions as well as right ones and living with the consequences of both. If Japanese budo leaders really feel we're ready for that, then they ought to say so. If American budo organizations are not ready for self-government in the opinions of Japanese leaders, then those leaders ought to make that clear, too. And whatever decision they make, they ought to be willing to live with the consequences.

47

Kiai

What is this *kiai* business all about?

It's the shout we make in karate, you insufferable bore. You going to make a big deal of a simple shout? Such replies tempt. Don't fall for it. In fact, few concepts play a more fundamental role in the budo than does kiai. Those who dismiss it so cavalierly and who fall into the temptation to consider the kiai as nothing more than a "karate shout" are apt to be dismissed themselves.

The concept is profound. While modern budoka tend to have a very narrow definition when they use the word, kiai is much broader in scope. Invariably, the average karateka refers to kiai as the vocalization of spirit or concentrated energy exercised in the martial arts. When a classical martial artist uses the same term, however, he more often uses it to refer to *intent*, or volition. A common criticism from a teacher engaged in a two-man kata with his student will be that "You don't have good kiai." Sometimes, this comment will be made at the commencement of the kata, when the two are closing the distance between one another. They haven't even gotten within range of each other. The karateka observing from the side might be confused at this. He, after all, saw only two people walking toward one another, perhaps armed with practice weapons. Nothing overtly "combative" has occurred. There has been no shouting or sounds of any sort. How can the teacher be criticizing kiai at this point? The answer is that within the koryu, the classical combative arts, kiai can mean, as I have said, a state of mind. The teacher sees that his student is not fully committed to what is about to happen. His kiai is weak, or unfocused. While it may be confusing, this is the wider (actually *deeper*) meaning of the term I would encourage karateka and other modern budoka to add to their vocabulary. Teachers, in particular, may find it useful. (Note: kiai, in this sense, cannot be adequately translated as "concentration." It isn't the same. Kiai as it is used in koryu dojo means more "an awareness coupled with a specific intention." It's shorter to say kiai.)

Kiai is a good word to describe the demeanor of the karateka as they move from their mutual bow into free-sparring or a prearranged exchange of techniques. Watch this very carefully. You can see a range of mental states at this moment. Some karateka will have a look of anticipation, others will try to "psyche out" an opponent, others will have some trepidation in their manner. Often, especially in dojo where significant emphasis is placed on the sporting aspects of sparring, you will see a pair of karateka begin their bout by a "settling in," as both feel out the other's intentions. (I have always been mystified at those who advocate "lots of free-sparring" as the gateway to mastering real life combative situations; this is one reason why. Aside from schoolboy encounters in the park, I can't think of many situations involving life-and-death encounters that include this little "warm-up" period where combatants dance and bob about.) What is the proper kiai for the commencement of a match? Something the more advanced karateka should think about.

Most well-read budoka know by now that the actual vocalization of kiai varies widely among the various classical combative systems of old Japan. It's possible, in many if not most instances, to identify a koryu simply by listening to the sounds. Katori Shinto ryu has its *Haw! Hutt!* and *Hooh!* Yagyu Shinkage ryu has a long, drawn out *Haaaahh!* Sometimes there are esoteric reasons for the exact sound, having to do often with the koryu's connections with Shingon Buddhism. More often, these particular audible kiai are believed to have an efficacious effect on a specific movement, coordinating weapon, spirit, and body. Less well-known is that Okinawan karate experts also used different kinds of vocalized kiai.

Even less well-known—and this is unfortunate for the karateka bent on perfecting his art—is that different kata call for different kiai. If you have ever seen a performance of the Okinawan stringed *shamisen* or other kinds of music from Okinawa, you may have heard the protracted *"Iiiiooo!"* that signals the start of the playing. If you have ever been around Okinawan construction workers or others engaged in strenuous activities, you'll have heard the peculiar *"Hawt!"* they give when a short, intense burst of energy is needed for lifting or pushing. The karate master Yabu Kentsu once used those sounds as examples of the range of kiai that should be implemented by karateka. What he was saying, in effect, was that the various actions of karate demand different emphasis in kiai. This is not to say that, for instance, a front kick requires a different vocalized kiai than a reverse punch. We're not talking about sounding like a one-man opera as you perform a kata. Instead, we're proposing the notion that the sound you make is more than incidental to what you are doing physically. This, I think, was Yabu's point and it is one overlooked by the modern karateka, for the most part.

Modern karate teachers rarely talk about the subtleties of kiai because they are unaware of them. They resort to bland generalities like "Just copy the sound your teacher makes" and hope the students will not embarrass them by pursuing the subject further. However, the greatest barrier to their understanding may be that failure to consider how the sound of their kiai interacts with their actions. "Make kiai when you have a point of focus," the average teacher says. Okay. But what is the focus during a movement when you're grabbing an attacker? Does a "big," expansive technique have a different kiai than a short, quick one? (This is one area where Japanese karateka, imposing their native idea of a decisive kime or focus on an Okinawan art, have diluted the original art.)

Kiai is just a "karate shout"? Yeah, sure. Remember to shout really loudly, though, because you'll be wading into the shallows of the art and those who are swimming in its depths might have trouble hearing you.

48

Yuyo (Critical Distance)

A tale is told of a duel fought by Yagyu Mitsuyoshi Jubei. Jubei was a rather swashbuckling sword master of the early 17th century in Japan. He was the second headmaster of the Yagyu Shinkage style of martial arts. Jubei was visiting the home of an influential lord in the capital of old Edo. While there, he was approached by one of the daimyo's vassals, a samurai who requested a fencing match. The duel was not to be a deadly one, conducted with sharp steel blades and meant to end in death. It was merely a test of skills that was proposed, a contest with blunt wooden swords. There was an element of something close to sport in these matches, which were popular in those days, although there were no actual rules other than those agreed upon by both parties, and injury was a very real possibility.

Jubei agreed to the contest. Jubei was the sort of fellow, to be honest, who probably agreed to any such contest that was proposed to him. He was of a straightforward temperament, never hesitant to uphold the traditions of his family school. By the time of this duel, though, he had, through some tribulations, learned that prudence could be as much a mark of the warrior as ability with the blade. So we can imagine that it was a Jubei eager to meet a challenger, but one also careful not to inflict needless damage. The impromptu match was held in the lord's garden. Gripping their wooden swords, the pair faced off. In duels of this sort, there were usually two styles of engagement. Either the participants would move about or remain almost still for long, long periods of time, searching for a psychological as well as a physical opening to attack, or they would, in an eyeblink, jump in and execute attacks. The slow matches could be boring for spectators, while the fast were usually finished so quickly that those watching never even saw what had happened. The duel between Jubei and the lord's samuari was the fast kind. Almost immediately, both swordsmen attacked, their weapons clattering together. They were still for a moment, then Jubei stepped back and bowed. But his opponent merely gripped his bokken more tightly and squared his stance. Jubei responded by once again taking up a combative posture himself. In the second duel the bokken clashed again, and again Jubei retreated and bowed.

"Another stalemate," commented his opponent.

Jubei shook his head. He looked at the daimyo who was watching the contest. "What did you see here?" he asked.

"They were both draws," the lord replied, concurring with Jubei's challenger.

Jubei shook his head. "It is unfortunate then," he said. "Neither of you understands the true principles of swordsmanship."

It is easy to imagine, of course, what the reaction of the lord's samurai would be. Angrily, he accused Jubei of trying to talk his way out of the shame of having drawn in matches that Jubei, as a famous martial artist, should have won. He demanded a fight with *shinken*, actual swords. Jubei tried to talk the man out of it. Even if there is only the intent to show superior ability, a free-for-all fight with shinken was a serious matter. (It is beside the point of our story here, but this incident is a perfect illustration of how situations can get out of hand, even for the expert martial artist. Put yourself in Jubei's place. A day that has begun with a simple social visit to an acquaintance has suddenly, without the slightest provocation on your part, turned into a moment when you face death, meeting it or dealing it out. The martial artist today who finds himself "just teaching a lesson" to someone in a confrontation which is not really serious should contemplate Jubei's circumstances here.) Jubei warned the challenger of the danger he faced. Nonetheless, the samurai was adamant. Jubei took up his sword.

One more time the two faced each other. Once again they came together and struck in what appeared to be a simultaneous motion. This time, however, it was the challenger who moved back. Blood soaked the front of his kimono. He staggered, and he fell into a heap, dying. Jubei was left standing in the garden alone, examining a sword cut he had received through the fabric of the outer layer of his kimono.

"The outcome of a real fight is determined by a distance of no more than one *sun*; sometimes less," Jubei wrote of the incident afterwards. He was referring to a measurement in Japan, one still used today sometimes, that equals a little more than an inch. (For practical purposes in the dojo, we traditionally measure a unit of sun as the distance between the second and third joints of your first finger. Acupuncture practitioners use a similar method in finding appropriate points on the body for treatment.) What Jubei was writing about is referred to in the specialized vocabulary of the martial arts as *yuyo.* Yuyo can be construed to mean an "interval of grace," the space that quite literally separates life from death. For such a sobering concept, the average budoka nowadays hears relatively little about it. And while he may encounter the concept if not the word itself in the training hall occasionally, it is likely his instruction in yuyo is haphazard and fragmentary.

If you want to see what yuyo is *not*, attend a typical karate tournament. You will see punches focused ten inches or more away from the intended target. Unfortunately, you may also see blows poorly focused with no regard for yuyo *through* the target, resulting in broken noses, bruises, and other injuries. What martial artists sometimes call "lack of control" is in reality, a lack of understanding or mastery of yuyo. Neither budo competition nor unrehearsed "free-sparring" can teach yuyo. It is developed primarily through prearranged sequences of practice, attack, and defense. In karate, this is called *yakusoku kumite,* an exchange of strikes and responses. In other martial Ways it may be known as *sotai renshu;* training with a partner in multiple techniques or kata. You punch; your partner cannot move away. He must accept the attack without flinching, trusting you will stop at the correct distance. He learns courage and composure; you learn how to focus your attacks exactly where you want them. Both of you are exploring yuyo.

Just as competition does not produce a sense of yuyo, neither will that sort of training where strict attention to it is not constantly maintained. Let us use the example of karate once again. You are practicing a three-step exchange of techniques which require you, say, to make three consecutive attacks. Perhaps they are *jodan,* or "upper level" punches, which your opponent parries, one after another, and then allows you to complete the final punch. But "jodan" is a vague term. Karateka often announce the attack to their partners, "Jodan" and then begin without much thought as to *exactly* where those strikes are to be aimed. Chin, nose, throat, where is your target? If you are just striking in the general vicinity and without a concise distance, you are not practicing yuyo, nor are you really doing budo. You are dancing, or exercising, perhaps. And that kind of activity has its rewards, true. But it is not a confrontation with the fine line between life and death that is the essence of real martial Ways.

Yuyo is the physical manifestation of that line. To strike, not just powerfully, but with focused accuracy, not two inches away from the target or so close that you are actually hitting it, but precisely where you wish the focus of energy to be.

Yagyu Jubei lived in the duel he had with the lord's vassal and in many other encounters with the sword, because he understood the importance of yuyo. He and his challenger both struck at the same time, but his mastery of distancing was so perfect that while his opponent cut the silk cloth of Jubei's outer clothes, Jubei cut flesh. He lived—and the challenger died—by the margin of one sun, a space, as I said, about the length of your finger between the second and third joints. In practice it is one sun that should be the distance remaining between your opponent and your attack at its completion. No more, no less. Yuyo. A most critical distance, indeed.

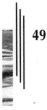

49

Thoughts on Learning

"It took me almost ten years in the dojo to learn how to learn," I once heard a budoka say. Interesting comment. Most of us come to the budo with at least some schooling behind us. We assume we know how to learn and that the real task is mastering the material before us: the techniques or the kata or the coordination required. We don't often consider that the actual ways in which we assimilate what is presented to us have a tremendous impact on our progress. *How* we learn in the dojo is at least as important as what we learn. And so here are three strategies I'd suggest for improving how you learn.

Learn to be flexible in your perspective. In his book on martial strategy, the legendary swordsman Miyamoto Musashi wrote about the "Rat's Head and Ox's Neck." He warned here that in a battle you can become too focused on this or that little detail. You risk becoming too involved in a small part of the conflict, without seeing the overall situation. Learn to pull back mentally, he advised. Look at the bigger picture. This is directly applicable to learning a technique. When a teacher is demonstrating an intricate movement, a joint lock, for instance, the students will be fixed on the minute manipulations of the hands or fingers. They assume this is the crux of the technique and direct all their attention there. They miss, when they adopt this method of learning, the broader action. The teacher's body shifting may be what makes the technique work. Get that shift down and you have the fundamental for that specific technique as well as, probably, many others. In general, especially when you are first introduced to new material in the dojo, focus your attention on the broader aspects rather than finer details that might need polishing later on.

You will often see a skilled teacher appearing to gaze off absentmindedly in the distance when he's supposed to be observing class. True, he may simply be bored. If he's good, though, more likely, he's deliberately focusing his look past the student. Try this. You will miss some of the particulars of what you're looking at. But, like the teacher, you will see some aspects of movement, especially, that you wouldn't notice otherwise.

Remember too, that the opposite can be true. Watching the action unfold on the whole battlefield gives you a general picture. But you gotta be careful of that fellow slipping up behind you to cut you in half. Similarly, there are times when you must focus on very minor, technical details. Find a balance. Avoid concentrating too much on one method of learning.

Be willing to appear stupid. This is a bit extreme, admittedly. But what I mean is that you must be willing to sublimate your natural ego and your desire to have your teacher believe you are competent. Often, a student will be stuck at one spot in a kata, for instance. He knows the entire sequence, but he's not able to get past that spot. The teacher comes and begins to demonstrate. As soon as the teacher gets to the student's stuck spot, the student says, "Oh yeah! Now I remember!" Fine, the teacher says, "Show me." More often than not, the student will make it past that stuck spot—and get stuck again a few movements later. Trust me. If a teacher begins to demonstrate *anything* for you, do or say nothing that will stop him before he wants to. Watch everything he offers, even if you're convinced you know it better than he does. If you don't you're apt to be embarrassed a second time when you still can't remember the technique. And more importantly, you will have missed an opportunity to see a senior perform.

In a similar situation, the student will be practicing and the teacher will say, "*Sono mama!*" ("Stay where you are!" or "Freeze!") It's natural to want to let your teacher know that you know what you're doing wrong. So, when he tells you to freeze you will have a moment to think and be tempted to move your hand or leg or position or whatever, into the place where you think it ought to be. This infuriates a couple of the teachers I know and I can understand why. Often, your self-correction is not a correction at all. Which means the teacher has to ask you to go through the movement again until you get to where your original mistake or practice point was. He has to correct your correction before he can get to the correction he wants to make. You can see where that would get on his nerves after a while.

If a teacher commands you to stop, do it. Freeze immobile. Many times, he will want to physically move you into the correction. He may want to show you why the way you're doing it is wrong. And at least if you stop completely when he tells you to, you may take some satisfaction in having done *something* right.

Discern between learning based on past experience and being open to new experience. I once saw a student being taught a new kata with a long staff. The sequence of movements he was working on was very similar to another kata. But there was a significant difference, a change in the grip. The student assumed he knew the sequence. He assumed it was exactly the same as the one he already knew. So the teacher, in a lighthearted mood, kept going over the sequence, watching the student follow and make the same mistake, smiling and shaking his head and doing it again. To those of us who had the luxury of watching, rather than being under the pressure of performing the kata, this was an illuminating lesson. Do not assume you know what is being taught just because it may look like something you've learned before.

Of course, an essential part of learning is building on to what you already know. You will never progress at all if you can't rely on what you have learned in the past. But you must avoid becoming too reliant on what you already know. One sees this constantly at seminars or other teaching situations where students may be exposed to entirely new arts. If you have a chance to observe one of these, it's worthwhile. You will see students who are learning tai chi, for instance, coming from a long background in karate. Unable to see the new art through anything but the filter of their karate experience, they come up with a weird hybrid. They have not learned how to get beyond their past experience and open up to a new one.

As my friend observed, learning how to learn is not an easy process, nor one that can be mastered quickly. But it is vital for the training of the martial artist. It is a skill you should constantly seek to improve.

50

Where Do You Stand?

There are, and this is clear to even the complete neophyte who has just entered the dojo for the first time, a number of differences between the combative disciplines of Japan and the West. Some of these diversities are in the contrasting philosophies, or the strategies of arts as different as, say, boxing and karate, wrestling and aikido. Some of the distinctions occur in the application of actual techniques. And some of these differences are representative of all three. A good example are the variations in posture or stance taken by the Western and Japanese martial artist.

In the majority of Western fighting arts—boxing is the obvious example, fencing provides similar evidence—the exponent faces his opponent nearly sideways, presenting to the front his leading shoulder. Both boxers and fencers assume this stance; it provides them with numerous advantages in the ring or on the fencing *piste*. Turning to the side protects the fighter's vital organs, which are grouped along the center line of the body. This was particularly important to the medieval swordsman in Europe. His bladed weapons were most frequently designed to thrust. He had to protect himself against the threat of linear strikes that were coming, pointed end first, directly at him. The boxer rotates his stance to protect and defend his body and head. His stance also allows for the full range of one of his weapons (primarily his fists and arms) to come into play in the space between his body and his opponent. The Western-style wrestler tends to face his opponent a little more squarely, but he will still keep one side shifted forward, to make a more difficult target.

Anyone familiar with these Occidental fighting arts will notice immediately, however, that Japanese karateka and kendoka and aikidoka take a different kind of stance preparatory to fighting. Rather than turning the torso away, they all face almost fully forward at an opponent. Their postures are not at all exactly similar, and there are several different terminologies to express subtle differences. But generically, we may think of their postural approach to confrontation as *hanmi*, a Japanese word that means "half-facing," with their torso twisted just slightly, but with the hips and head facing to the front.

According to the dominant Western strategy of a protective posture, it would seem that hanmi gives up too much. Hanmi allows an opponent access to vital areas of the body's midline. (By some quirk of evolution for which I am sure biologists will have a reasonable explanation, many of the "goodies" on the human body are located along a line down our middles. So protecting this line is a significant factor in any fighting art.) But while the exponent in hanmi exposes these targets, remember that he also compensates by having both arms (and legs) available for protection. It is a trade-off in the combative sense: give more to your enemy, but simultaneously, bring more weaponry into position to protect yourself or to launch offensively.

The contrasting approaches to stance in Eastern and Western fighting arts pose many interesting questions. There is little doubt, for instance, that the oblique posture of the fencer originated from the predominant use of the swords of Europe. These blades were primarily grasped with one hand. The Japanese katana is a two-handed weapon. It requires a more fully frontal stance to be wielded effectively. Consider, however, a question which will occupy the hoplologist. A hoplologist is a specialist in the field of anthropology whose interest is in a study of the weaponry and fighting of different cultures. These are the sorts of things he wonders about: did hanmi evolve as a result of the two-handed katana, or did the katana develop as it did because of a preference for a style of fighting in Japan where combatants faced one another squarely? The same question could be asked of the Western fencer and his primarily single-handed blades. Which came first? The specific weapons, or the manner in which they were used? And why? Did hanmi evolve because of the Asian physio-cultural emphasis on the hips and a low center of gravity, while the more upright oblique stance preferred by the Western combatant came about as a result of our emphasis on the power and development of the upper body? These are questions beyond this short discussion, to be sure. As is the question of why many less-than-traditional karate tournaments are filled with contestants who squat at each other sideways, their bottoms sticking out as they hop around in stances that render completely unworkable a vast percentage of karate's techniques and strategies. The stances of these contestants are not like those of a boxer, nor like those of the competent karateka. They resemble some kind of weird hybrid, boxers trying to perform karate or karateka attempting to box. The results are rather pitiful.

It is fascinating to consider the many ramifications of the two different postures of East and West. To me, the most significant are the very different approaches to combat itself that are revealed in hanmi and in the Western oblique stance. Let us consider two of those differences. First, the postures of the boxer and the fencer are geared to the contingencies of single combat and combat in a relatively confined space. They are designed too, for extended encounters. The boxer and the fencer try to wear down an opponent, to peck and hunt for his targets, gradually overcoming or weakening the enemy until the *coup de grâce* or knockout can be administered. There are, though, no such equivalent expressions in the vocabulary of the *kenshi*, the Japanese swordsman. His strategy was not to carve up his opponent, but to finish the encounter decisively, with one stroke. Ikken hisatsu—one strike kill—is a term and a way of thinking that the karateka and other budoka learned from the kenshi.

From the kenshi the karateka and aikidoka and kendoka also gained the concept that they must accept the possibility of multiple opponents. This is the second distinction between hanmi and the oblique posture of many Western fighting methods. The budoka cannot afford to "spar" with an enemy, or to "square off" with him. He must strike and subdue, and then move on, cognizant of another enemy even if none is immediately apparent. This mentality as much as anything characterizes the attitude of the Japanese martial arts as different from those of the West.

While they may look similar to the untrained observer, and while both may be fighting postures, something very different is implied by the combatant who assumes hanmi and one who takes up the oblique stance. Each has strengths and weaknesses. Each encourages the application of different attacks and defenses. The serious martial artist should consider this carefully, and reach at least two conclusions. He should decide that the basic stance taught by his art is one way, but not the only way to stand in combat. He should also make an intensive study of the other methods. Secondly, he should understand that while it is fine to be ecumenical in one's attitudes, there are crucial differences between the many different fighting arts of the world and the methods of one cannot necessarily be integrated into another . . . at least not without losing a sense of where it is one stands.

51

Honto no Haikai (Proper Perspective)

When I was a schoolboy, I spent a lot of my weekends out among the lime-stone crags and cliffs of the Ozarks, rock climbing. My climbing partners and I were minimally armed with only the most basic of gear—this was back in the sixties when monofilament nylon rope was still something of an innovation in the climbing world. A lot of the equipment that's standard among climbers today was not even dreamed of in those days. Even so, we spent many contented hours working our way up rock faces, far above rambling streams, wooded hills, and farmlands that stretched out below us.

This was also a time when few people were involved in outdoor activities like hiking or climbing. But occasionally in our adventures we'd run into others who shared our interest. Less occasionally, we'd run across the fanatics.

The "climb-*kichigai*" we referred to them; the "climb-crazy." They were the sort who did not pursue climbing as an activity or a sport. For them, it was an obsession. Their passion for it burned so brightly that any possible outside inter-est was fried to a crisp before it could ever be realized. These were the sorts of guys who skipped weddings or funerals to go off climbing instead. The climb-kichigai may have been on the knife-edge of starvation, but if it was a choice between buying a side of beef or purchasing a new rope, well, there wasn't any choice at all. They'd have scraped the bottom of the peanut butter jar and bought the new rope. The climb-kichigai lived to climb. Everything else came in a very distinct second in their lives. In rattletrap cars, hitchhiking even, they would head out to tackle some new route, leaving friends, spouses, jobs, and school behind.

Anyone who has been involved with a sport like climbing knows the sort I'm talking about. Skiing has its share of fanatics. Their numbers can be found in the worlds of surfing, marathon running, and so on. It shouldn't be surprising that the budo has its own contingent of kichigai. Typically (but not always) they are young, male, and they can be spotted instantly in the field, recognized by an intense, white-hot drive to train. Often they will be taped in half a dozen places to mark injuries they've suffered. But they will still be at the dojo for every class, and they are apt to remain there long after everyone else has gone home for the night.

These budo-kichigai are frequently held up as models for other students to follow. "Look at Joe-san over there," a teacher will remark with some pride. "Arm's broken and his mother died yesterday, but he just quit his job at the supermarket so he'll have more time to train." And over there indeed is Joe. Whacking away at a makiwara, on his sweat-splashed face beaming a beatific smile of joy. You look at Joe and you're trying to remember where you have seen similar expressions, faces lit with a similar kind of inner light. And then it occurs to you that you've seen that expression in religious art. Saints smile like that.

There may be a few saints among the budo-kichigai. But it's been my experience that many dojo fanatics are anything but worthy models for the rest of us. Their practice is not the kind of practice we want to do, not as a training for the wider perspective of life. Their practice is an end to itself. They mistake the dojo for real life. Their training becomes a substitute for the interactions, the responsibilities, and the relationships that real life imposes and promises.

If the budo-kichigai has a good sensei, he may be made to see the folly of his attitude and his approach to training. His sensei will show him that life exists outside the dojo, that in fact, the dojo is a training ground for meeting that life. The lessons applicable to the action in the dojo must, if they have any meaning or value at all, be worthwhile in meeting the situations one encounters every day outside of it. Punching the makiwara a couple of hundred times a day doesn't have much relevance in daily life, true. The determination and consistency of that kind of practice, though, is instrumental when tackling challenges far removed from the confines of the dojo: in keeping a steady job, finishing one's college degree. Yet if the persistence of martial training never goes beyond the dojo it has pathetically little meaning. It is like learning to write letters, practicing them over and over, but never putting them together to form words.

More importantly, the teacher will point out to the budo-kichigai that in his single-minded pursuit, he is neglecting obligations and depending on others to take care of them. Look behind the budo-kichigai and chances are you will see a long-suffering spouse or parents footing the bills. They will be feeding him. Taking care of his clothing, his insurance, his transportation. All too often they are thanked by his ignoring them. His training is too important, he tells himself (if he thinks about it at all) to be distracted by considerations of gratitude. Or consideration of anyone or anything else at all, for that matter. The budo-kichi-gai will rationalize. "Look at all I am giving up in order to train," he'll say. But the truth is, it's those around him who are doing the giving. He is only taking. And that kind of selfishness, no matter how noble the motive, is still just self-ishness.

Training in the dojo is essential to the budoka's search for a more meaningful life. If he approaches that training as a substitute for life, though, his reward will not be at all what he expects. There is no self-perfection at the end of that road. Only the most bitter and meaningless of existences.

52

Sempai & Kohai (Seniors & Juniors)

There were in old Okinawa, two karateka who had trained together for many years. One was named Taro no Yabu, called that because his family had lived in the little village of Yabu, on the northwest coast of the main island of Okinawa, longer than any other. His friend was named Kenyu, but since his childhood, everyone knew him as Kame, "The Turtle." The nickname came about partly because Okinawans have always been fond of them in general, nicknames that is, and because Kame was quite large and powerfully built and he had the careful and deliberate movements of a sea turtle.

Although Taro and Kame were close friends and both were students of the same karate teacher, their personalities were entirely different. Kame, a sweet potato farmer, was very easygoing and had a gentle manner that allowed him to get along with virtually everyone who knew him. Taro, a fisherman by trade, was known for his quick temper. He was easily drawn into arguments, especially among his friends.

Taro would never have resorted to violence to settle his frequent disputes in his hometown. In fact, all it took was a companion teasing him about his anger, and he would realize the foolishness of it all and tend to laugh off the whole incident. But once a month, when he loaded his catch of dried fish on his back and made the trip to sell it in the nearby trading center of Nago, his self-control was not so complete. In the inns where he and the other fishermen would convene after selling their catch, he would have to hear only a single insult about the place of his birth, and he would feel compelled to defend it. That was unfortunate for Taro, because his village of Yabu was the butt of numerous jokes in the region. The feet of Yabu women were regularly and not flatteringly compared to those of a mud heron's. A northerly wind was said to carry the stench of an outhouse in summer to every place south of Yabu. Inevitably, someone would make a crack about his home village, and Taro would answer with a challenge.

Because Taro's reputation as a karateka was every bit as deserved as his renown for his temper, the offending party would usually end up apologizing for his remarks—provided he was still upright and capable of speech after the encounter. But after two or three of these fights, word of Taro's behavior got back to his karate master in Yabu. He warned Taro that if another such episode occurred, Taro would be expelled as a student.

The warning by his teacher came at an inopportune time for Taro. Scarcely a week before, he had made one of his regular trips to Nago. While there, he had managed to get involved in an altercation with the town's most skilled karate exponent. Taro had defeated the man with little difficulty. The problem was that the townsfolk of Nago were angry that their local hero had been beaten by a simple country bumpkin like Taro. They made it clear that on his next visit to Nago, a score or more of them would be there to greet him and to make sure he learned more respect for their town.

So when the day came for Taro to take his load of fish to Nago again, he prepared for the trip with a heaviness in the pit of his stomach. He knew he had to do business in the town, and he knew the threats were serious ones. It was inevitable he would have to fight. Before he left Yabu, he went to Kame, his friend and senior in the karate group, to ask his advice.

Kame sat without moving or talking as Taro explained his predicament. With the studied deliberation of the turtle he'd been named after, he finally said, "Your family's welfare must come before your karate training. You will have to go to Nago to sell your fish. If you are attacked, you will have no choice but to defend yourself, no matter what the consequences will be."

Taro started out for Nago with Kame's words in mind. He arrived at the fish buyer's there, conducted the sale of his catch, and just as the sun was setting he headed back on the path to Yabu. With every single step he took on the winding trail, he breathed more easily. He had not seen a single one of the crowd that had sworn to get him. Still, he could not forget that the path ahead of him was deserted this time of the evening and surrounded on both sides by a thick hedge of jungle vegetation. The canopy of trees above hid the moonlight. Taro had to make his way along with a lantern. It was dark and quiet and lonely and when it seemed darkest and quietest and loneliest, he heard it. Not quite a scream, not quite a howl. The noise was a mournful, awful wail.

There are no really dangerous animals on the island of Okinawa except for the *habu* snake. But Taro knew there were spirits that inhabited the region. And so when the weird cry burst from the darkness the hair on the back of his neck bristled. He was terrified. Then the wail came again along with a crashing in the jungle. Whatever was making such a noise, he knew he was at its mercy. And so he resigned himself to his fate, said a prayer, and moved forward again towards Yabu. Again and again as he walked along, he would hear a rustling in the jungle, and then the wail. It seemed to him as though it took forever, yet eventually he made it home. Taro was so badly frightened by the experience that later his children would remember that it was that very night when their father's hair began to turn grey, even though he was still a young man.

The following morning Taro was telling his wife about the terror he'd encountered, when Kame came by on his way to the fields. Kame listened to the tale, and when his friend had finished, he shook his head and got up to leave.

"At least," said Taro's wife, "if the monster scared you he must have also scared away the men who were going to fight with you."

"Yes, indeed," agreed Kame. "It is amazing how frightened of such creatures the men of Nago can be." And then Kame threw back his head and from his throat came the same awful wail Taro had heard the night before.

The Turtle's ingenious way of protecting his friend is an example of a special relationship within the budo that is known in Japanese as *sempai-kohai*, or "seniors and juniors." When you enter a dojo, those already training there are your seniors, your sempai. Those who come after you have joined are your kohai, or juniors. And so it remains, regardless of the rank you may eventually achieve, your respective ages, or experience. Easy enough to understand. Except that in a traditional dojo it is never just that simple. For there is the matter of *on*, or "obligation," that is to be reckoned with, a concept that will have a great deal to do with the budoka's training. By being your senior, by helping you, by kicking you when you are lazy, by acting as advisor, coach, and confidant, the sempai assumes a tremendous responsibility. He assumes a sense of on to his junior. The kohai who has been tutored and taken care of by his sempai incurs a considerable on to his senior as well, since he is indebted to the sempai for the sempai's kindness and attention.

The concept of sempai-kohai and the notion of on that is inherent in these relationships springs from the well of feudal Japanese culture. It is a culture that was based upon class distinction and clearly delineated lines between one's inferiors and superiors. Even in modern Japan, it is not hard to find evidence of these distinctions—in schools, in the world of business, even in friendships. Juniors are careful to respect their seniors and to depend upon them. They seek the help of seniors in gaining promotions at work, in arranging introductions to the opposite sex, in countless ways. In return, the sempai takes his position seriously, not as someone who has the power to lord it over the kohai under him (although this may sometimes be the case), but as a guiding influence whose role may last a lifetime.

The sempai-kohai system plays an important role in budo training. In the old days, a master usually had only a few students. And so he could afford to spend a lot of time with each of them. In today's budo dojo, there may be dozens of students. The teacher can instruct on a close basis only those who have reached the higher levels of experience. The rest of the dojo must depend upon their seniors to act as guidance counselors and as coaches, initiating them into the sometimes confusing ways of the budo. The sempai's responsibility may include actual instruction from time to time. More typically, his role is to take care of the junior by answering his questions, coaxing him on when he is doubtful or discouraged. The kohai, in turn, makes every effort to return the kindness of his senior, treating the sempai like a respected older brother or sister. Both are constantly mindful of the obligation each has to the other.

The sempai-kohai relationship in the dojo allows a junior to begin the long process of maturation in the budo. It encourages the senior to develop attitudes of helpfulness and leadership that are necessary for mastery. So in a mutually cooperative and productive way, the lives of both sempai and kohai are bettered.

That is not to say, however, that these relationships are always smooth. For the junior, it may seem that his every movement is criticized. Even outside the dojo he finds his behavior under the watchful eye of the senior. I have seen promising young budoka abandon their training because they refuse to accept this situation, confusing it, I suspect, with the shallow and essentially pointless sort of "hazing" that characterizes adolescent social cliques in American colleges. And from the sempai's perspective there can also be resentment, a feeling that his kohai is an unappreciative child.

This impatience with the sempai-kohai system is nothing new, but then again, neither is the system itself. The relationship between seniors and juniors has been a cornerstone in the building of a budoka since before the Kame's clever imitation of a jungle devil frightened away the would-be assailants of his kohai. In spite of its apparent drawbacks, it really works rather well. If you are a beginner in the budo, remember that. Listen carefully to the comments your sempai make. Their experience has been hard won. If you are a more advanced practitioner, keep in mind that training is only a part of your purpose in the dojo. There are kohai in need of your guidance. It is up to you to set the example.

Traditions

At Christmas a couple of years ago, my wife gave me a book on traditional Japanese woodworking tools. Anyone who has seen me wield even so much as a hammer would immediately guess this book was not a "how-to" manual. Giving me an instructional text on woodworking would be like providing a St. Bernard with lessons in trigonometry. It was, instead, a compendium of the tools and equipment used by the *shokunin*, the craftsman-carpenter of pre-modern Japan. The book detailed descriptions and the use of all sorts of tools employed by the shokunin as he made or repaired everything from houses and massive temples to delicate sliding *shoji* screens. Some of the tools would be recognizable to the Western woodworker: hammers and planes. Others are decidedly different from their Western counterparts. Chisels are shaped more like spades. Axes look more like gardening hoes. Some saws resemble long spatulas with teeth on both sides. And there was an assortment of tools for which there simply are no equivalents outside Japan. Weird, spiky chisels. Ripping saws that looked like the jawbone of a *Tyrannosaurus rex*.

Only a few decades past, a book like my Christmas gift would probably have had few readers. Industrialized societies all over the world a very short time ago placed little value on pre-modern arts and crafts, on traditional ways of doing things. Back during the sixties and seventies, advertisers were quick to use words and phrases like "high tech," "instant," and "new and improved," for everything from laundry detergent to surgical procedures. Such an emphasis is understandable. The finely wrought precision of the shokunin craftsman took years of apprenticeship to perfect. A construction worker putting up a new house could be trained in a matter of months. Flawlessly matched joinery and hand-finished woodwork might glow with life and last for centuries, sure. But plastic and stainless steel were convenient and affordable.

Indeed, it was and is hard to argue with these changes, in some sense. Those who long for the days when homes were built by master craftsmen can conveniently forget that the average person in those days couldn't begin to afford that craftsmanship and was more likely to live in what we would now consider squalid hovels. (In 1958, the Japanese government sponsored an enormous study of life in rural Japan to determine the quality of life and discovered that more than 70 percent of the home kitchens in non-urban Japan had dirt floors. An even greater percentage had no running water and relied on public wells.) Romanticizing a past that was full of graceful architecture and superbly handmade furnishings is easy to do when we do so at the remove of a modern and affordable and comfortable and safe lifestyle. The first time I walked into a *minka*, an old Japanese farmhouse, I was captivated. Massive, ship-timber beams. Vast spaces of tatami. Reed-thatched eaves. Minka are unquestionably among the most aesthetically pleasing architectures man has ever created. As I wandered through the house, though, a companion started pointing out some blunt realities. Those beams overhead were darkened because minka had poor ventilation; the smoke from the cooking fires blackened all the wood in the upper parts of the house. Those wide open spaces of tatami meant heating the house during Japan's cold, humid winters would have been a nightmare. And those beautiful thatched roofs were supporting entire civilizations of mice, sparrows, and other creatures with which one should expect to share home. I still dream about owning a minka. But I don't dream about them so much I forget to turn up the thermostat when my house gets a bit chilly.

And so our enthusiasms for the ways of the past must be tempered and balanced by an appreciation for the real progress humankind has made. Without that appreciation and realization, waxing nostalgic about the virtues of traditionalism leans a little toward the hypocritical—especially when I am doing so in words composed on a computer and read by you as the result of the latest in printing and bookbinding technology. Nevertheless, for all its benefits, one legacy of the Industrial Revolution is no doubt that decoration and affectation have too often replaced beauty and elegance, that accessibility has superceded efficiency, that fashion has become confused with style.

In response to some of the unhappiness created by a society too focused on what is new, there is evidence many are looking, in some aspects of their lives at least, to the past. In Japan, the *Mingei-kai*, the Folk Crafts Association, was founded to preserve traditional arts and crafts. Potters and other artists have attracted large followings; tour groups from other parts of Japan and abroad now regularly make pilgrimages to several villages that are bustling with native crafts-men and artisans. In the West as well, a return to the old ways has become popular. An editor of mine left his job last year to learn to build frame and timber houses. Interestingly, at least to me, is an observation of the same trend in the budo. It wasn't that long ago that all we heard about were eclectic forms of com-bative arts, modernized and update composites created by those who patched a little of this with that and who "updated" the old stuff to make it relevant. Karate was all about flashy uniforms and acrobatic, free-form kata and such.

Yet despite the glamorous appeal of carpeted training halls and musical kata and tournament egotism, some students were not satisfied. They looked elsewhere. They discovered, in time, the past. And as with other serious artisans, they discovered in that past something profound. They began to see why the budo are called martial *art* and how they can become a Way of life.

What I've observed here is simply a reiteration of the introduction of this book, of course. Tradition has achieved a new sense of importance in the lives of many people. Budo, a traditional approach to the martial Ways, is to some degree a part of that trend. Today, there are thousands of people in every country on the planet who are absorbed not by learning something new, but by trying to find the values and merit of what is old. That's great for a codger like me, who is always happiest when I'm looking backward. Even as I applaud this trend, however, I have to wonder. Have we returned to traditionalism simply because we have exhausted every other form of entertainment, every other avenue in the search for getting what we want? What is it that we really mean by the "tradi-tions" of budo? Once, in a conversation with a now long-departed editor of a martial arts magazine, he identified an action film star as a "traditional karate guy." What makes him traditional I wanted to know? The editor's response: "Oh, he wears a white uniform."

If the outer trappings of traditionalism are what attracts us to these older ways, if we turn to them merely because we've become jaded with all else that is offered in the marketplace, the results of trying to follow these old and estab-lished paths are going to take us nowhere worth going. Adopting the template of a classical, traditional approach to budo (and so to life itself) has many implica-tions we need to consider. It's like moving into one of those minka folk houses. You'd better be prepared for some discomfort, for some expenses, for some changes in your life that will be far from easy. You'd better know what you're getting into and you should be clear as well on exactly why you want to make such an extraordinary move.

I have tried to shed some light on some of the aspects of the traditional martial Ways here. It is up to the individual, however, to make sense of his own journey along these Ways and to decide if such a trip is worth it. I can't; no one else, teacher or senior in the dojo or author, can provide for you the motivation to discover what it is that makes the budo so compelling and to keep you going. You have to find it for yourself. In closing, I can only offer one analogy that often occurs to me when I am thinking about my own practice of the martial Ways. I think of it too, whenever I am around a waterfront and the boats found there.

If you go to a public or private boat dock, you will see that most of the watercraft tied up or moored there are made of plastic or fiberglass or aluminum. They are functional, to be sure. Each is mass-produced, made on assembly lines literally by the hundreds of thousands. They are uniform in design, indistinguishable one from the next. But if you are fortunate, you may also see a handcrafted wooden boat. If one's there, you'll see it right away. A wooden boat stands out, though in a quiet way. It is lively and graceful, even if it's held down to the dock by mooring lines. It has lines and a symmetry of shape that could never have come from just a draftsman's blueprints. The designs for these wonderful boats, it was once explained to me, come more from the exacting craftsmanship and long experience of a master boatbuilder. They are unique and individual, and even if a builder is using blueprints, certain characteristics will creep into the design, necessitated by the properties of the wood and other materials as well as by the personal desire of that builder. The lines and shapes of such a boat are called in the trade, "fair curves." A fair curve is a shape that cannot be entirely measured by instruments. It has a quality we can sense, but one that can't be duplicated, no matter how skilled the builder, not unless he has pursued a similar apprenticeship in creating these waterborne masterpieces. Fair curves come from more than technical boatbuilding skill. They come from the spirit.

The budoka, I think, if he is really dedicated to his craft, searches for the fair curves of the martial Ways. In his training and in his life, he seeks that intensely personal mastery that defies description, but which can be sensed and seen immediately. Through the old, time-tested traditions of the budo, he finds meaning and substance in living today. Budo, in this sense, *is* a traditional art, in name and practice. And anyone who follows it with that motivation can truthfully call himself a martial *artist*, seeking to find within himself, his own fair curves.

Also by
DAVE LOWRY

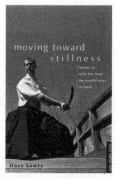

0-8048-3160-2

$16.95
Paperback

MOVING TOWARD STILLNESS
*Lessons in Daily Life from the
Martial Ways of Japan*

Moving Toward Stillness is a collection
based upon Dave Lowry's magazine articles
from the past decade, mostly from his
highly regarded column in *Black Belt* magazine. Written from an almost Japanese
perspective, it offers an entertaining and
informative view of the martial arts. Topics
explored include entering the martial way,
making the pursuit of traditional Asian
martial arts a part of modern Western life,
the paradoxes and conflicts such a path
inevitably generates, how to adapt to the
mindset necessary for true mastery of a
foreign art, and much more.